A
PSYCHOLOGY
FOR LIVING

A
PSYCHOLOGY
FOR LIVING

**Personal Construct Theory
for Professionals
and Clients**

Peggy Dalton *and* Gavin Dunnett

JOHN WILEY & SONS

Chichester · New York · Brisbane · Toronto · Singapore

Copyright © 1992 by Peggy Dalton and Gavin Dunnett

Published 1992 by John Wiley & Sons Ltd,
                   Baffins Lane, Chichester,
                   West Sussex PO19 1UD, England

All rights reserved.

No part of this book may be reproduced by any means,
or transmitted, or translated into a machine language
without the written permission of the publisher.

Other Wiley Editorial Offices

John Wiley & Sons, Inc., 605 Third Avenue,
New York, NY 10158-0012, USA

Jacaranda Wiley Ltd, G.P.O. Box 859, Brisbane,
Queensland 4001, Australia

John Wiley & Sons (Canada) Ltd, 22 Worcester Road,
Rexdale, Ontario M9W 1L1, Canada

John Wiley & Sons (SEA) Pte Ltd, 37 Jalan Pemimpin #05-04,
Block B, Union Industrial Building, Singapore 2057

Library of Congress Cataloging-in-Publication Data

Dalton, Peggy.
    A psychology for living : personal construct theory for
  professionals and clients / Peggy Dalton and Gavin Dunnett.
        p.   cm.
    Includes bibliographical references and index.
    ISBN 0-471-93549-2 (pbk.)
    1. Personal construct theory.   2. Personal construct therapy.
  3. Personal construct theory—Popular works.   4. Personal construct
  therapy—Popular works.   I. Dunnett, Gavin.   II. Title.
  BF698.9.P47D35   1992
  150.19'8—dc20   92–15127
                                                            CIP

British Library Cataloguing in Publication Data

A catalogue record for this book is available from the British Library

ISBN 0-471-93549-2

Typeset in 11/13pt Palatino from author's disks by Text Processing Department,
John Wiley & Sons Ltd, Chichester
Printed in Great Britain at The Alden Press, Oxford

For
Bill and Mike

CONTENTS

PREFACE

Gavin Dunnett died in October 1991 at the age of forty-two. He edited two books and contributed chapters on personal construct psychology to a number of others. *A Psychology for Living*, however, was the last thing he wrote. We shared a respect and enthusiasm for Kelly's work, which led to a very happy and stimulating collaboration.

We wrote this book in an attempt to make the ideas of George Kelly accessible to those who have little or no formal psychological training but feel the need for a coherent framework for their understanding of themselves and others. Kelly's theory is increasingly applied in a wide range of settings, especially those concerned with therapy, education and other areas where such understanding is essential. Many professionals, be they therapists, teachers, social workers or personnel managers, find that this approach both enhances their work with clients, pupils, students and fellow workers and helps them personally to deal more effectively with the difficulties and dilemmas which face them in their own lives. Just as important, we wanted to write so that clients and anyone who might be helped by reading this could become their own "psychologist".

The theory is complex and there is no intention to reduce it by over-simplification. We hoped, however, that by a process of interweaving theoretical ideas and practical examples we might convey the essence of what to us is the most meaningful view of personality to be evolved so far.

The structure of this book is based on the kinds of question often asked by colleagues, students, clients and friends. Whether their questions are about the theory or practice, or about how it might help them personally, the interest is clearly there and we attempt in the following chapters to provide a resource for answering them.

Peggy Dalton *and* Gavin Dunnett
April 1989

ACKNOWLEDGEMENTS

Our warmest thanks for all they have taught us and for being who they are to Don Bannister, Fay Fransella, Miller Mair and Tom Ravenette. Other colleagues, students and clients have also joined us in many experiments from which we have learned much of what we have tried to express in these pages. To George Kelly himself we are most indebted of all.

1

WHAT IS THIS THING CALLED PCT?

INTRODUCTION

The Psychology of Personal Constructs (1) was first published in the United States in 1955. It could be described as a *magnum opus*, running as it does to two volumes and some 1200 pages. It was the culmination of more than twenty years of clinical and theoretical work and was written by a psychologist called George Kelly.

It is probably useful at this stage to try and clarify the different names around for this psychology, and the abbreviations that go with them. As mentioned above, the volumes originally published were called *The Psychology of Personal Constructs* and so we often refer to Personal Construct Psychology, and this is abbreviated for ease of reference and speech to PCP. When talking or writing of the theory which Kelly outlines specifically in his book, we refer to Personal Construct Theory, or PCT for short. In many ways these two terms are interchangeable and indeed are used indiscriminately. To be precise, however, and Kelly himself was very precise in his writing, the theory refers to the explicitly stated postulate and corollaries which provide the framework for this view of personality, while the psychology is about how it all works in an individual. We will try to keep to this distinction throughout the book, and will use the abbreviations PCP and PCT as described.

The other abbreviation often encountered is "Kellyan". Personal construct psychologists are often called Kellyans, rather as some psychoanalysts are called Freudians, or client-centred therapists are called Rogerians. This use of the name of the original perpetrator of a theory or approach has the merit of reminding us who did originate it, and provides a conveniently short handle as a description. Conversely, it does tend to provide an image of a band slavishly following the teachings of one specific genius, or great man. We are sure Kelly himself would have been either utterly appalled by such a prospect or hilariously amused. He himself wrote that he saw his theory as merely being the starting point of many new journeys which might well produce new and better theories in the future. While his optimism about a new and better approach does not seem to us to have been fulfilled yet, there have been many developments and elaborations of both theory and psychology since 1955. So although "Kellyan" is used to refer to an approach in line with PCT, it does not necessarily mean that it was written by Kelly himself.

WHO WAS GEORGE KELLY?

George Alexander Kelly was born in Perth, Kansas, on 28 April, 1905. He was the only child of a Presbyterian minister and his wife. His father had turned to farming because of ill-health. His early education was in a small country school, and he subsequently attended four different high schools over a period of four years in Wichita, Kansas. Kelly's parents were religiously devout, and he was brought up with traditional Midwestern values of hard work and puritanical views on drinking and dancing.

From high school, he went on to Friends University where he studied for three years, and then followed this by a final year at Park College from which he received his BA in physics and mathematics in 1926. His original career choice had been in engineering with a particular interest in aviation, but he had been active in inter-collegiate debating during his studies, and this influenced him towards a career in more social than mechanical areas. He moved to the University of Kansas, studying educational sociology principally, supported by labour-relations, and wrote a thesis based on a study of the distribution of leisure-time activities of workers in Kansas City. He was awarded his MA in 1928.

For the next few months, Kelly had a wide range of jobs including conducting classes in public speech for the American Bankers Association and Americanisation classes for a group of recent immigrants, and acting as a part-time instructor in a labour college in Minneapolis. He then became a member of the faculty of a college in Sheldon, Iowa, where he met his wife, Gladys. They were married in 1931 and had two children. In 1929, he had been awarded an exchange scholarship which he spent at the University of Edinburgh studying education in which he earned a bachelor's degree. He returned to the States in 1930 to enrol as a psychology doctoral candidate at the State University of Iowa and was awarded his PhD in 1931 for a dissertation on common factors in speech and reading disabilities.

What is interesting about this background is that, before Kelly took up his first post in academic psychology at Fort Hays Kansas State College, he had had a wide range of experience of strikingly different subjects. Initially mathematics and physics, an interest in engineering, sociology and labour-relations, education and finally psychology. As you get to know his theory, you may find it interesting for yourselves to look at aspects of its structure and presentation and speculate to what extent these different influences on the early Kelly emerged in his later work. One further reason for presenting you with this early information about the man is, as will be elaborated later, that the theory is fundamentally *personal*. So the theory itself is the *personal* production of its author, and while it may not help you to understand its intricacies any better, it certainly may make some of them more interesting!

Kelly stayed at Fort Hays for twelve years. In his paper, 'The Autobiography of a Theory' (2), he describes how these years in the poverty-stricken dust-bowl of Kansas forced him to examine his views and change his approaches. He was initially the only psychologist in the area, and found much of his formal training unhelpful to those he was trying to work with. He re-read Freud, whom he had initially rejected, and this time found more of interest and relevance. As time went by, he began to feel that his clients were more affected by prolonged drought, dust storms and economic vicissitudes than by the libidinal forces as outlined by Freud. He also began to experiment with giving increasingly bizarre interpretations and found that the clients responded more to the way the therapist presented these than to the content of them. It is from this time that he began to develop his ideas which, with many modifications and regular discussions and arguments with students over the years, would culminate in his publication of 1955.

During World War II Kelly worked as a naval aviation psychologist, moving to the Aviation Branch of the Bureau of Medicine and Surgery of the Navy in Washington DC where he stayed until 1945 when he was appointed associate professor at the University of Maryland. One year later he was appointed professor and director of clinical psychology at Ohio State University where he remained for the next twenty years. In his time at Ohio, Kelly completed his major theoretical contributions to psychology as well as reorganising and administering the graduate programme in clinical psychology.

In 1965 he was appointed to the Riklis Chair of Behavioural Science at Brandeis University, Massachusetts, but he was only to have a year there before he died on 6 March 1966.

In addition to his career as teacher and theorist, Kelly served as president of both the Clinical and Counselling Divisions of the American Psychological Association; he was instrumental in developing the American Board of Examiners in Professional Psychology; and he was latterly interested in international affairs, travelling around the world with his wife during 1960–61 on a grant from the Human Ecology Fund applying PCP to the resolution of international problems.

Leaving aside his achievements in the field of education, training and professional enhancement of clinical psychologists in America, Kelly is principally remembered for the development of personal construct psychology which has continued to be elaborated and developed over the ensuing years. Its history has been documented by Neimeyer [3] and, although it has not had as much influence as some other contemporary theories, it has remained alive and flourishing. In many ways, it was a theory ahead of its time, and its ideas and approach are more suited to the world today, and the scientific and human approaches extant now, than they were in the 1950s. Thus, although over thirty years have passed since the publication of *The Psychology of Personal Constructs*, the ideas remain fresh, vital and stimulating. At least, we think they do, and we believe that despite needing to struggle with new philosophical ideas, a highly explicit structure, and the redefining of some common words, the underlying approach is fundamentally human, warm, optimistic, and, above all, personal.

ELEMENTS OF PERSONAL CONSTRUCT PSYCHOLOGY

In writing about, or attempting to describe, PCP there are three main elements which need to be explained. The first of these is the philosophy which underpins the theory; the second is the "person-the-scientist" metaphor which Kelly uses to describe any individual's way of making sense of his or her world; and the third is the structure of the theory itself, with its fundamental postulate and accompanying corollaries. Although this sounds like a vast and very complicated task, the bones of it all are not difficult to grasp, and are essential to getting to grips with the application of the theory as described in later chapters.

At this early stage, can we just encourage you not to panic or give up prematurely. The remainder of this chapter and Chapter 2 are heavy going. If you begin to feel swamped, go on to Chapter 3 and read a bit more from there. You can always come back for another go at the more academic parts later. They are important for a full understanding, but not so important at this stage as to put you off personal construct psychology for life!

The Philosophy

It is unusual for a theory of personality to begin in the realm of philosophy, but in fact this is really quite essential. Unless there is some understanding of the world in which the individual operates psychologically, it is very easy to make assumptions about that world. Indeed most psychological theories make philosophical assumptions about the world in which they operate, but generally they do not do so explicitly.

Kelly, on the other hand, quite explicitly brings up this issue at the outset, defining his philosophy as that of "constructive alternativism". This imposing title is rather daunting but not really that difficult to understand. It comprises Kelly's convictions about the universe and about man's relationship to that universe. He wrote:

> "The three prior convictions about the universe ... are that it is real and not a figment of our imaginations, that it all works together like clockwork, and that it is something that is going on all the time and not something that merely stays put". (1)

He goes on, in relating life to this universe, to say:

> "Life, then, to our way of thinking, is characterised by its essential measurability in the dimension of time **and its capacity to represent other forms of reality**, while still retaining its own form of reality". (1)

So what does this mean in rather simpler language? Essentially, that there is a real world out there. It exists, is interconnected, and is in continual motion. An individual living being is always trying to grasp hold of that real world but in fact only constructs his own version of it. However, the construction that he makes of it is infinitely variable. A huge range of alternative ways of construing/making sense of the same event are available. However, to that individual, whatever construction is made is real to him.

In one of his most often quoted paragraphs, Kelly wrote:

> "We take the stand that there are always some alternative constructions available to choose among in dealing with the world. No one needs to paint himself into a corner; no one needs to be completely hemmed in by circumstances; no one needs to be the victim of his biography. We call this philosophical position constructive alternativism."

An individual, indeed all individuals separately, develop their own personal view of the world and what goes on in it. For each individual there is a huge range of alternatives only bounded by the rules he imposes on the system itself. And those rules, being created personally, can be altered by personal choice also. Equally, the personal view of the world created by one individual may to a greater or lesser extent be similar or different to that created by any other individual, inherently *personal*.

Person-the-Scientist

In order to elaborate this philosophical position of constructive alternativism, Kelly put forward the metaphor of person-the-scientist. In fact Kelly proposed this metaphor as "man-the-scientist" but with modern thinking about sexism we have felt it appropriate to change it. Scientists are people who examine particular phenomena, and endeavour to come up with theories about how that particular phenomenon works, or what it actually is. They make predictions based upon their theories, and carry out experiments to see whether these predictions are correct or not. If the experiment provides a positive response, it is regarded as validating all or part of the theory which spawned it, while if a negative response is produced, it is regarded as invalidation, and the theory has to be re-examined to try to explain the problem.

Kelly's metaphor was that essentially this was the type of activity all people were engaged in. Everyone was making their own theories about the real world out there. They were doing this in order to be able to make predictions about their future. Once these theories had been formulated, and predictions made, people went ahead on the basis of these and discovered from their experimentation whether or not they worked out in practice. If the predictions worked, that part of the theory would be incorporated into the individual's psychological system. If not, re-evaluation and re-organisation would need to take place.

For example, a young person who has always been shy is invited to a party for the first time. From listening to her sister's stories of parties and seeing them on television she has a picture in her mind of a crowded, noisy room, full of people all talking brightly and ignoring her because she is quiet and dull. She is terrified, but she goes. If what she has anticipated turns out to match her experience of her first party, her theory will be proved and, probably, she won't want to try again! If, however, she finds that it is not a noisy affair, that several people talk to her and seem to find her interesting, she will hopefully reconstrue and her anticipations of parties will be modified in future.

Reflexivity

One important point to grasp about this metaphor is that it applies to *everyone*: you reading this book; ourselves as we write it. It applies as much to the counsellor providing counselling, as to the person receiving it. Psychologically, we are all conducting the same kind of activity. Thus the process by which we all live our lives psychologically is governed by the same set of rules, although the content is unique and personal to each of us. This notion of the applicability of this approach to ourselves as well as everyone else is known as "reflexivity", and for many of us is one of the great attractions of PCT. What it means is that there is simply a way of understanding how all humans operate psychologically, whether they do so effectively, or whether they get into difficulties. To take a mechanical view, it is important to understand how a machine operates normally before you can begin to make sense of why it has broken down, and how it may be mended. So PCT provides us all with a psychological system of normal functioning, and then, within that framework, looks at what happens when different parts break down, or are misused. Finally, when normal functioning and the cause of breakdown are fully understood, then and only then are the various ways of returning the system to normal functioning considered.

Thus the philosophy relating life to the universe, together with the metaphor of person-the-scientist and the idea of reflexivity, acts as the basis for the explicit theory which follows in the next chapter.

2

THE THEORY ITSELF

As we have proposed, everyone has "theories" about everything, whether they are explicitly verbalised or not. All psychological approaches to personality have theories behind them, though some have never been fully expounded. Of all of these, PCT is one of the most meticulously spelt out. It is complex, it is consistent in its detail and, to us and many others, it is essential to the application of everything we do when we work with it. (Later on we shall be discussing its usefulness in other aspects of our lives.) This is why we have chosen to devote time and space to describe it in this chapter and shall be referring to it constantly in later ones.

PCT consists basically of a "fundamental postulate" and eleven "corollaries". Although this is a very formal presentation and rather unusual for theories of personality, it acts as a basic structure from which the clinical and other theoretical parts of the approach can be derived. It is probably not important for you, the reader, to attempt to grasp all the ramifications of these statements at this stage. We feel, however, that it is important to run through them so that they can begin to feel familiar, and can be referred back to when particularly relevant features occur in later text or discussion.

A. THE FUNDAMENTAL POSTULATE

The fundamental postulate states that:

"A person's processes are psychologically channelized by the ways in which he anticipates events."(1)

Being *fundamental*, this postulate is not open to question. For the purposes of the rest of the theory, it is taken to be true. That is not to say that it cannot be argued with, but if it is, it ceases to be a postulate for this theory, and is merely one amongst many possibilities. Meanwhile, let us make the assumption that what it states is so. This enables us to build the remainder of the theory upon it.

Kelly discusses each of the words he uses in this fundamental postulate, and it is worth following his lead here as they each hold specific significance.

Person. This focuses the theory on the individual as a whole, rather than any part of him/her, any group or any particular behaviour. It indicates a holistic approach to the individual, seeing him as a complete entity.

Processes. This indicates that from the psychological perspective, the person is continually in motion, and it is this motion itself which is being considered. This avoids the need to suggest an entity such as mental energy to work upon an inert person. The person is a behaving organism,

> "not temporarily in a moving state but is ... a form of motion". (1)

Psychologically. Here Kelly states that

> "when we use the term psychologically, we mean that we are conceptualizing processes in a psychological manner, not that the processes are psychological rather than something else". (1)

It would theoretically be possible to look at a person's processes physiologically, or sociologically, but for the purposes of this theory we are going to look at them psychologically.

Channelized. This suggests that the processes operate through a network of pathways. This network has a clear structure but is also flexible. Thus it both facilitates and restricts the person's range of action.

Anticipates.

"Anticipation is both the push and pull of the psychology of personal constructs" (1) wrote Kelly. This accounts for the predictive and motivational elements of the theory. The network of pathways looks to the future so that the person is enabled to anticipate it.

Events. The person is ultimately trying to anticipate real events—anticipation is not carried out merely for its own sake, but so that future reality may be better represented.

"It is the future which tantalizes man, not the past. Always he reaches out to the future through the window of the present." (1)

Perhaps it would be a good idea for you at this stage, before going on to look at the corollaries to the fundamental postulate, to run over in your head some of the areas we have already covered. There is, after all, rather a lot of new material there, and much of it has probably been presented differently, or maybe you have never seen yourself as understanding any philosophy at all. Why not run down the checklist below, and if you cannot think clearly about a particular part, go back and read through it again. Remember that this is not meant to be a test of your learning ability, or your intelligence, or indeed of anything judgemental. It is simply that our experience is that many people often find their first introduction to PCT difficult, and frequently feel foolish or stupid if they don't grasp it all at once. An occasional pause to review in your own head what we've just covered avoids the possibility of grinding through the rest of this book wondering what on earth we are really on about.

1 Philosophy of constructive alternativism
2 Metaphor of person-the-scientist
3 Reflexivity
4 The fundamental postulate

B. THE COROLLARIES

We now move on to the next large amount of theory. Again it is not important for you at this stage to remember what they are, or what they all mean. But at least you can begin to recognise some of the issues they represent, and you can refer back to them when other aspects of the psychology are discussed in relation to them later on in the book.

There are eleven corollaries in all. A corollary is essentially a statement which follows on from one already made (in this case the fundamental postulate) as an immediate inference, deduction or consequence. In other words, once the fundamental postulate is accepted for the purposes of elaborating the theory, then these eleven further statements can also be accepted as following on automatically from it. They also serve the purpose of elaborating specific elements of the theory which are important in its application to and understanding of an individual's personality. Together with the fundamental postulate, they provide the framework on which the whole of the theory rests, and which can then be used to understand how you or I use the theory in practice for ourselves, and in our worlds. So together the fundamental postulate and the corollaries are rather important. However, like the fundamental postulate, they are written rather abstractly. We will try as we go through them to give some specific examples of the implications of each different corollary, but do not worry if all does not seem totally clear. As you progress through the book, new ideas and implications will be presented at different times, and these will refer back to the corollaries, so that by the end of the book, hopefully, you will feel fully familiar with them even though you will still have many questions left to answer.

1. The Construction Corollary

"A person anticipates events by construing their replications." (1)

This corollary reiterates the notion that anticipation is the principal motivation behind an individual's psychological processes. It also introduces for the first time the idea of "construing". Construing means essentially "placing an interpretation upon". In order to make sense of an event, an action or a situation, a person attempts to construe it. Erecting a structure within which what is observed takes shape and takes on meaning for the individual.

It is important at this stage to emphasise that construing is not the same as "thinking". We construe as we look, listen, touch, taste, feel and move. As we perceive something visually or audibly we are interpreting what we see and hear. As we taste, say, that mouthful of tea, we are giving it meaning probably without any "thoughts" in our heads at all. And, as we shall show later, some of our constructions of events never reach our heads at all but remain as feelings, sensations that we scarcely notice. Lastly, action or behaviour itself is very much part of the construing process. If we reach out to pick something up we are, in a sense, testing out a "theory" as to what it will be like when we hold it. If we approach another person with certain feelings we are again checking out our expectations of them.

If construing is about erecting structure which allows a personal interpretation to be made about that which is observed, then "constructs" are those pieces of scaffolding comprising the structure itself. Constructs are a means of discrimination between observed items (usually called "elements") in terms of similarity and contrast. In any given series of elements, a person looks to see what aspects are similar to one another, and are dissimilar to others. Each construct created is bipolar—that is to say it has what is known as an "emergent pole" and a "contrast pole". Both emergent and contrast poles together form the construct on the principle that one cannot tell that what one observes is anything specific without having something to contrast that with. Would you recognise black if you didn't have the ability to contrast it with white for example? All constructs have contrast built in to them. Be careful though, it is *contrast* that is built in, not *opposite*. Often people think that constructs are composed of opposite poles, and then assume that they must be verbal opposites. This is not so.

The first thing to remember about constructs is that they are the personal creation of the individual, and may therefore be totally unique to that person. So the contrasts are those which that person finds most useful in construing the world about him or her. These contrasts may or may not be useful, or even understandable, to another person. Thus one person may have a construct of

LIGHT contrasted with DARK

while someone else may have had a construct of

LIGHT contrasted with SHADY

Constructs are what individual people make for themselves. It is therefore incumbent on anyone else to understand the personal meaning of those constructs for that individual, not try to impose their own constructs. But more of this later.

The second thing to remember about constructs is that they are a psychological entity which we often use words to symbolise, but the words we use merely represent the construct: they are not the construct itself. Indeed, as you will discover in Chapter 4, there are many constructs which have no verbal labels for one reason or another. They may be non-verbal constructs or preverbal constructs.

Either way, it is easy to begin to think that words and constructs are the same, just as it is to see construing as the same as thinking. They are not.

The third point is one of annotation. You will remember that constructs are about similarity and difference—contrast. For ease of reference, the verbal label given is usually written with the word versus between the two poles. Thus for the examples given above, the usual annotation would be:

LIGHT versus DARK

or

LIGHT vs DARK

While *how* a person construes is by distinguishing similar from dissimilar, and creating a resulting structure of constructs through which meaning and anticipation can be developed, *what* the person construes is what Kelly calls the replication of events. Put simplistically, this means that as a person progresses through life, he looks for recurrent themes occurring in the endless flow of living. One can imagine driving along a motorway, keeping your eyes open for signposts and landmarks that tell you where you are, and which you can recognise in future to help you anticipate what comes next. It is the recurrent nature of elements that allow them to be construed.

> It will probably have become apparent already that this corollary is very important, especially since it brings up the notions of construing and constructs for the first time. Before you go on to the next, try checking in your own head that you know what we mean by "construing", and what a "construct" is, and what its characteristics are.

2. The Individuality Corollary

"Persons differ from each other in their construction of events." (1)

This corollary is relatively straightforward in that it states simply that people differ! While this seems an obvious statement that could be put down to common sense, it is nonetheless the embodiment in the theory of the philosophy of constructive alternativism. The latter states that there are an infinity of different ways in which the world can be construed; this corollary states that individual people will use different constructions out of that infinity, even to construe what is apparently the same event. Furthermore, because their constructions may be different, so it follows that their construction systems will be different also.

Therefore any individual may anticipate different events, thus leading to different construction systems, and also may anticipate the same events differently. The process is continuous and circular. *Because* they have different construction systems, *so* they will construe the same events differently. *As* they construe the same events differently, so they will tend to anticipate different events, and so on.

The process is rather like two people setting off on a journey together. They travel down the road until they reach a T-junction. One takes one route while the other chooses the alternative. As each of them progresses, so they come across an infinity of other junctions each of which they have to make choices about. Each of their experiences of where they have been and what they have seen is therefore different, but their paths may have crossed at points on their route, and they may have seen the same views but from different roads and perspectives.

The individuality corollary is the basis upon which the "personal" appears in personal construct psychology. If each person differs from every other in their construction of events, so it follows that although they may use common ways of organising those constructions, the meaning attributed will be unique and individual. Anyone trying to understand another person has, therefore, to try to make sense of the constructions that other person is making of his life.

3. The Organisation Corollary

> "Each person characteristically evolves, for his/her convenience in anticipating events, a construction system embracing ordinal relationships between constructs." (1)

As we pointed out in the discussion on the individuality corollary above, people not only differ in their construction of events, but also in the way in which they organise these constructions. This corollary is about that organisation.

Remember that the basic item in the structure is the construct. The fact that it has two contrasting poles is irrelevant here because you cannot have one pole without the other. So constructs are the basic materials out of which this organisation/structure will be created.

Let us for the sake of argument imagine that a construct is equivalent to a piece of scaffolding. Everyone must have seen around the huge variety of shapes and areas covered by scaffolding, either outside or inside buildings. Scaffolding has the amazing ability to be used to get at any shape in almost any direction. Yet if you think about it, it is joined together by extremely simple joints to make complex and different shapes.

The organisation of a construct system is rather similar. Constructs are linked together in "ordinal" relationships, rather like the spars of scaffolding. They don't just float in an amorphous psychological sea, they relate to one another. And like a system of scaffolding, some are down at the bottom of the system, others are further up and so forth. The constructs near to the bottom (and this is just a way of looking at it—there is not an actual bottom or top) are more concrete, while those at the top are more abstract.

This is because the relationship between constructs works up and down as well as laterally, as in a scaffolding system. Just as a single piece of scaffolding at the top of a structure may be being supported by hundreds of pieces at the bottom, so a single highly abstract construct at the top of the construct system may be related to hundreds of more practical and concrete constructs at the bottom, through various levels of decreasing abstraction in between.

There are two sets of terms you need to remember in relation to this organisation. They are "Subsuming" and "Superordinate"/"subordinate".

Within any construction system there are many levels of relationships, the lower ones more concrete and the higher ones more abstract. Where one construct hierarchically applies to more other constructs than a lower construct, and is therefore more abstract, it is said to subsume that other construct. Also, because the relationship between the two constructs is ordinal, the subsuming construct is said to be superordinate to the other. Conversely, the subsumed construct is said to be subordinate in relation to the construct which is subsuming it.

This may be a rather complex set of ideas to get hold of so let us think back to our analogy of the scaffolding. All the pieces of scaffolding are jointed together to form a framework—these are equivalent to the ordinal relationships between constructs. The pieces of scaffolding up top are "up in the air" and are equivalent to more abstract constructs, while those at the bottom are "down to earth", and are equivalent to more concrete constructs. Each level of the scaffolding subsumes those pieces it is jointed to underneath it. The top piece is superordinate to everything below it; while the next piece down is subordinate to the top piece, but superordinate to everything below it; and so forth down to the bottom-most piece which is subordinate to everything. In fact we tend to have far fewer abstract/superordinate constructs than concrete/subordinate ones, so the scaffolding construction would tend to look pyramidal in shape. A two-dimensional model is shown in Figure 2.1. In Figure 2.1, Construct A subsumes Constructs B and C, and is superordinate to them. Constructs B and C are subordinate to Construct A, but in turn subsume Constructs D and E, and F and G respectively, and are superordinate to them. Constructs D, E, F and G are subordinate to everything in this part of the system.

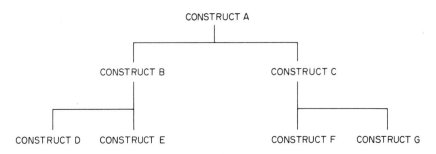

Figure 2.1 Hierarchical relationship of constructs

By now you should have some idea of a construction system extending up and down, with constructs subsuming others, and being superordinate or subordinate to one another. You should also have the idea that as one climbs up through the system, the atmosphere becomes more rarefied, i.e. more abstract, and that there are fewer constructs at these levels, thus producing a pyramidal picture.

Unfortunately, that is not all. Two other points need making at this juncture, although you will find that some of the later corollaries also add information to this structure. The first point for now is that the structure is three-dimensional. That is to say, taking Figure 2.1, that while Construct A subsumes Constructs B and C, it may also subsume Constructs X and Y (not shown because in a different dimension) and so forth. Constructs B and C, however, may not be directly related to Constructs X and Y at all. Thus again, like the scaffolding structure, it extends in three dimensions.

In Figure 2.2, "successful vs failure" is at the top, the most abstract. This subsumes all the others underneath it. And you will see how they become less abstract as they go down with, for example, "is friendly" and "well-trained" at the bottom (not that this is as far down as we could go). Further, we can see that while "has good relationships vs doesn't relate well'; is subordinate to "successful vs failure" it is superordinate to "friendly vs unfriendly" and "listens to others vs only talks about self".

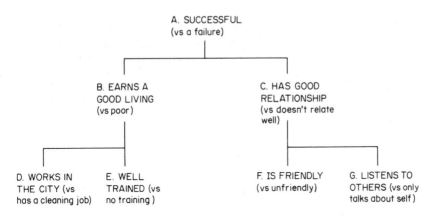

Figure 2.2   Example of construct hierarchy

Finally, the last point here is to remember that in fact a construction system is not static. It is perpetually being altered and amended by the person who is creating it. The analogy here is of the single scaffolder perpetually moving around the scaffolding creation, always trying to make it fit better, or extending it to cover another area. Ultimately it is his construction, for his use, to enable him to anticipate and understand better. And so it is continually changing as he alters it.

4. The Dichotomy Corollary

"A person's construction system is composed of a finite number of dichotomous constructs." (1)

You have already met the term "constructs" in our discussion of the construction corollary. This corollary merely defines constructs as dichotomous–that is to say that they have two contrasting poles, and states that any individual construct system is composed of a finite number of them.

In relation to the first part—that constructs are dichotomous— you will remember that constructs were used as discriminations between the similar and dissimilar. In order to define the two poles, a construct has to apply to at least three elements, two of which are seen as similar to one another, while the third is dissimilar. However, the similarity and dissimilarity has to be in relation to the same aspect that is being viewed. Thus looking at three turnips for example, two may be regarded as *small* and similar, while the third is by contrast *large*. It would make no sense to describe the turnips as *small* rather than *mechanical*. Such a construct would be of no help at all. A construct consists of *both* poles, and whatever it is discriminating between has to apply to the element upon which it is brought to bear.

The second part of this corollary relates to the fact that a construction system is composed of a *finite* number of constructs. Although there are an infinite number of ways of construing events, for any individual the system will only contain a certain number of them. His system is finite, although its capacity for alteration and change as time passes is infinite.

5. The Choice Corollary

"A person chooses for him/herself that alternative in a dichotomized construct through which he/she anticipates the greater possibility for extension and definition of his/her system." (1)

This corollary leads to what Kelly calls the "elaborative choice". If constructs are dichotomous, and we have agreed above that they are, then when considering any element in relation to a particular construct, a person must choose which pole of the construct is most appropriate in relation to that particular element (assuming that it applies at all—see "The range corollary" below). But that person must have some basis for making his/her choice, and the choice is made on the basis that it provides the greatest possibility of extension or definition of the system. Extension suggests that the choice allows further construing to take place to add to the anticipation for the future, and to add predictive parts to the system. In other words it tends to allow new matters to be considered, and leads to the system growing. Definition implies that the choice allows the system as it already exists to be confirmed, or redefined. Elaboration can be in the direction of extension or definition.

6. The Range Corollary

"A construct is convenient for the anticipation for a finite range of events only." (1)

This introduces the term "range of convenience". All constructs have a range of convenience which simply means that any given construct only applies to a specific group of elements. That is not to say that a person cannot try to apply a construct to an element outside its range of convenience for a variety of reasons, but it probably will not help in anticipation or prediction. Consideration of an underground train as *masculine* or *feminine* is of no use while you are waiting for it to arrive: a construct of *early* vs *late*, however, may be, as might one of *full* vs *empty*.

7. The Experience Corollary

"A person's construction system varies as he/she successively construes the replications of events." (1)

This effectively states formally what we mentioned above in the last paragraph of discussion on the organisation corollary.

Construction systems are not static, they are perpetually in motion. The person is *all the time* in the process of predicting and anticipating events, and incorporating into the construction system the results of these predictions and anticipations. Thus the system is always in motion, always being changed, altered, added to, subtracted from, re-arranged and so on. You are not given a construction system with which you are lumbered for the rest of your life, to do as well as you can with. YOU are always in the process of creating it, and although what you have already created now affects how you operate in your life, there is nothing stopping you changing it if you want to. Indeed as you go on experiencing day by day, hour by hour, even microsecond by microsecond, you are checking out your predictions, and using the results of all these experiments to alter and amend your system.

Of course, most people do not go in for wholesale change of their system all at once. They need a certain amount of consistency and stability to continue while they change some aspects of their systems. Major or enforced change may produce nasty effects on one hand, while an inability to contemplate change at all, or only in very minor areas may also cause problems. (See Chapter 5 entitled "What can go wrong?")

8. The Modulation Corollary

> "The variation in a person's construction system is limited by the permeability of the constructs within whose range of convenience the variants lie." (1)

This corollary, together with the experience corollary just discussed, is concerned with how a person goes about changing his/her system. They are the rules relating to its alteration, rather than its construction, or how one part relates to another.

> "A construct is permeable if it will admit to its range of convenience new elements which are not yet construed within its framework." (1)

The construct itself does not necessarily change, but it can be used to consider new elements, and can accept that there are new elements which are within its range of convenience and to which it can thus be applied.

Suppose that someone has been brought up to believe that "good people" are those who believe in God and go to church, whereas "bad people" are those who don't believe and don't go to church. As they meet more people, there is a possibility that they will change this construction. If "good people vs bad people" is permeable then as a construct it may be able to take in those who don't believe but help others, are warm and caring etc., on the good side and those who do go to church but are selfish, unkind, dishonest on the bad side. Someone whose system is impermeable will be less likely to change in this way on this or any other construct than someone whose major constructs have gradually allowed in new elements as they have developed.

9. The Fragmentation Corollary

"A person may successively employ a variety of construction subsystems which are inferentially incompatible with each other." (1)

Here we are going back to the way in which the system is constructed. We all know of situations which we choose to treat in one way even though we know that in another place or time we might deal with the same situation differently. The way we deal with someone at work, for example, may be quite different to the way we would deal with them in the pub on a Saturday night. Both are part of our system, but are inferentially incompatible.

A stronger illustration of this comes with a person who expresses very powerful beliefs, say, in the equality of all and yet, where his or her own family is concerned, this "equality" goes by the board. A firm supporter of the Labour party, perhaps, doing sterling work at election time, might nevertheless send their child to a private school to give "a better chance in life". When challenged, the clash between the two incompatible systems is obvious. One argument in protest might simply be that, come the crunch, "doing the best for your own" overrides the feeling that opportunities should be equal for all. A possible construct which could bind the two together at a more superordinate level might be "doing your best under given circumstances vs not making the most of the opportunities that are there". After all, they could only afford to send one child to that school.

Different subsystems can exist side by side, and be used at different times without necessitating changing the system itself each time and without necessarily being inferentially incompatible. A person may successively see himself/herself as workman, parent, son, gardener, and car-driver, each with its own characteristic behaviour which could be quite different each time. However, where these different types of behaviour produce conflict and are not resolvable, owing to the separate nature of the sub-systems, then fragmentation has occurred. Each of these would have a separate subsystem of constructs, subsumed perhaps under a superordinate construct of *human being* vs *alien* where the person chooses to see himself/herself as a human being.

10. The Commonality Corollary

> "To the extent that one person employs a construction of experience which is similar to that employed by another, his/her psychological processes are similar to those of the other person." (1)

Until now, we have emphasised how different individuals are. They anticipate differently, construe differently, organise their constructs differently, and use them differently. Individuals are unique. They build up their view of the world as they choose the different roads to travel down. The pattern of roads traversed and experienced by one person will always be unique to that person only. But there is nothing to say that two people cannot have traversed the same pieces of road, and seen the same view, and construed it in the same way. All that this corollary is pointing out is that where two people see things the same way, then in that aspect of their system, their psychological processes are similar.

There is a trap here, which will be discussed more fully in a later chapter. Do not forget that we are talking about constructs here, and not about their verbal labels. It is very easy to assume that if you hear someone talking, and using a particular word to describe something, they are using that word, and therefore the underlying construct, in the same way you would. This, more often than not, is not true, and leads to inevitable misunderstanding, and often subsequent acrimony. You have to check out what another person's meaning is, and compare it with your own, before you can say there is commonality between you. As you will see this is particularly important in relation to children.

11. *The Sociality Corollary*

"To the extent that one person construes the construction processes of another, he/she may play a role in a social process involving the other person." (1)

All the corollaries until now have been concerned with the processes going on in an individual person. Everything is *person*-based, seen from the eyes of one particular person, not generalised but kept at that level.

However, people interact amongst each other, so there has to be a way of seeing how that takes place, otherwise we would all exist psychologically as totally separate entities which we clearly are not. We do relate to one another, learn from each other, communicate with each other and so forth. This corollary sets out how that process is founded. In order to have a social relationship with another person, an individual has to begin to make sense of the construction system of that other person. Effectively it is a process of getting to know. The more one begins to understand/construe someone else's system, the larger the social role that one is likely to play in relation to them.

Note however, that we still remain individually based. I do not have to take on that other person's constructs, only understand them and this corollary makes no demand that the other person takes any steps whatsoever to construe my construction system.

All that is being said is that, if I bother to try, I will play a role in a social process involving that other person. If he/she also tries, we will both play roles in relation to one another which is likely to produce a far more satisfactory interaction.

This has been a long chapter to wade through with many new ideas, much new terminology, and several complex notions to grasp hold of. Do not worry if everything is not clear—it would probably be very boring if it was. Remember that PCP is a totally comprehensive theory of personality, and all the pieces of it ultimately link together. After all our years of working with and using PCP, both of us continually find new paths to follow in it, and new ways of understanding both it and its application. One final analogy for this chapter may help you if you are feeling confused.

Imagine you are considering buying a large old house. It has many rooms and staircases, an old bell wire system, internal and external windows, several stories, garrets, attics and cellars. The estate agent takes you round it all once, and then asks you what you think. Probably you have a general idea of the house; some aspects of it you have particularly liked and remembered, others you have already forgotten. You can't really remember which room came off where, or where that little back staircase led to. This chapter is a little like that house, and ourselves, as authors, the estate agent. You have just had a whistle-stop tour around the building and all is not clear. You probably do have a feel for it as a whole, though, and hopefully you are attracted to it, and want to explore it further, part by part and room by room. Eventually it may feel very familiar, and you will be able to find your way around easily, and you may wonder why you ever thought the geography difficult. If you decide to move in, of course, as we did many years ago, it will become more and more understandable although never less stimulating or interesting to be part of.

The chapters which follow will pick up many of the themes and issues only briefly raised above. They will endeavour to help you to explore and elaborate for yourself your own personal view of Kelly's theory. Good luck.

3

HOW DO WE COME TO BE AS WE ARE?

We must first make clear what sort of question we are attempting to answer here. It is not within the scope of a book such as this to philosophise on the origins of life or contemplate the mysteries of human evolution. Nor do we see it as our task to give a comprehensive survey of existing formal theories of early development. Since Kelly views "personality" in terms of the networks of personal constructs formed over time from the ways in which we make sense of ourselves and our worlds it follows that our main focus of inquiry should be on the theories people themselves have about how they come to be as they are. We shall look first then at some of the beliefs that are held about the influences governing personal development and the implications of those beliefs for much of what people do with their lives.

Before you read the following section, write down what you feel has contributed most to the development of your own personality.

Not everyone has thought to verbalise their own personality theories. But most of us have them at some level and it seems important to try to express them in some form as part of self-understanding. We have found in therapy that the notions emerging as significant to the individual are a central part of their philosophy of life, just as Dorothy Rowe (4) sees ideas as to what happens to us after death as crucial to the way we live. They can indicate whether there is a basic sense of freedom to change and choose or a person feels set on some predetermined course over which there is little or no control. You may have found, if you followed our suggestion, that several factors emerged for you. For many people one element seems dominant over all others.

SOME PERSONAL THEORIES OF DEVELOPMENT

It's in the Genes

Some people look to heredity and construe their past and future largely in terms of both the traits and fortunes of their parents and grandparents. They have a temper, a drink problem, a gentle disposition, will live until they are ninety because it's "in the family". Such ideas can't be dismissed and can help us to define ourselves and perhaps make some useful predictions or take mitigating action. But they can be limiting, threatening, even immobilising. Coming to view ourselves in this way can begin with the parents' need to define their children in terms of likeness to each of them and differences from one another. A mother sees her daughter as like herself and perhaps her own mother in being "sensitive" and easily upset. The other child is tougher, like father. Before long the two children are construed almost solely in relation to manifestations of sensitivity or toughness and are responded to accordingly. Unless they themselves come to challenge such labelling, the first has little opportunity to develop resilience, the second is inhibited from showing "weakness".

More threatening are the fears of inheriting the illnesses or blows of fate suffered by those whom we are taught we resemble. Some diseases *are* of course inherited but the fear of their onset can play a powerful part in a person's contracting them and even more in the way they respond to them when they do. In a family with a history of psychological problems it sometimes seems that a depressed, anxious even "psychotic" person has for years seen no escape from the familial tendency. To see oneself as "taking after" a parent who committed suicide can be terrifying and people may seek help when they near the age at which he or she died. The death in a road accident of a grandmother whom she loved and emulated led one young woman to confine herself to the house for years for fear of meeting the same end. To free themselves from such terrors a person may need first to review their whole philosophy of inherited predestination.

I was Born to It

In most cultures or contexts there are, of course, even more powerful constructions governing a person's expectations. If family or racial tradition has defined your role in life in advance there may be certain limitations to the choices you can make. While not denying the scope the individual has to make something personal of, say, being the heir to the throne, the eldest son and therefore a priest, the eldest daughter and thus responsible for ageing parents, the broad structure of life's course for many people is often laid down and accepted. On another level, men and women of all races are subject to role expectations and even in this day and age it may take some courage and imagination to elaborate yourself beyond them. A man may choose to stay at home and look after the children, a woman become a bishop, a black person challenge a whites-only establishment, someone of either sex find greater fulfilment in homosexual relationships. Such choices *are* made. But in general, more people than would care to admit it are at least partly defined by cultural and social expectations which are spelt out to us in various ways from the beginning.

The influence of religious teaching is, of course, all-pervading for many people. For some, the guidelines for belief and behaviour form a clear and reassuring structure. They know where they have come from, what they are here to do, and what will become of them when they die. This can lead to a powerful sense of responsibility to fulfil a specific role in life to the utmost or passive acceptance of "God's will", depending on how a particular person sees his or her place in the scheme of things. Others, born into a religious family or culture are torn by doubts and questioning and may feel compelled to reject religion altogether or reconstrue some of the basic assumptions passed down to them. Either way, such a struggle may represent the central process in their becoming who they are.

It was My Mother

In Western cultures in particular many see the course of their lives as entirely governed by the behaviour towards them of one person—most often their mothers, sometimes the father. For example, wondering why she had so little success with relationships and had achieved nothing in the way of a career, Janice came across a book which explained how a critical mother could ruin her daughter's entire prospects for love and success by stunting the growth of self-esteem at the outset. Suddenly everything fell into place. She had failed her exams because her mother did not want her to be happy. Janice carried this theory around with her for a long time, never questioning its validity, seeing herself as helpless in the face of such profound insight. In some ways it was a relief. She could not be held responsible for what happened to her. While she remained locked in this belief nothing could change for her. Indeed at some level she was working quite hard to prove that theory. It gave her the structure she needed to explain her lot.

Laura made something different of her mother's critical attitude towards her. Seeing the unhappiness her complaints, ill-temper and pessimism caused she set out to be as little like her as possible. She was "easy-going", concerned to please others, took whatever came to her with resignation. All of which made her a pleasant person to be with but cost her dearly in terms of her inability to express anger, inattention to her own needs and acceptance of whatever was thrown at her by others. Only when she learned that these two contrasting ways of being weren't the only possibilities was she able to acknowledge and express a wider range of feelings and relate to others on more equal terms.

Colin's father was domineering and possessive. He ruled his family of four sons and two daughters like a despot, making every decision, binding them chiefly by keeping them short of money or bribing them with gifts. At the age of sixteen Colin ran away from home, went to London and by various means, not all of them legal, set about making a living. He only made contact with his family to tell them of some lucrative deal he had struck or the wealthy girl he was about to marry. When he had a son he saw him as something with which to threaten his unmarried brothers. He would be the heir. Although in many ways a "success", Colin was as trapped in his theory as Janice and Laura. He had become what he was in defiance of what his father had done to him. But much of what he did was related to proving that he wasn't in his power.

In Colin's case there was the added factor of defining himself as different from his brothers and sisters, who remained under his father's thumb. The influence of siblings has received less attention than that of parents but it can, of course, be very powerful. A child may respond to an apparently favoured brother or sister by seeking to be as much like him or her as possible. They may try to excel in the same sports, the same school subjects, setting little store by qualities which are uniquely their own. They may strive to look and dress the same, even adopt the same mannerisms in an effort to find similar favour. Conversely, particularly where the parents have distinguished them, the child may elaborate differences—a girl become a tom-boy, for example, in contrast to a sister who is praised for her prettiness and sensibilities. This, as we have said, can be limiting to both, causing one to fear her more assertive qualities, the other to deny her femininity.

The influence of teachers and other older people in children's lives can sometimes be as strong, if not stronger, than that of parents in directing them along certain paths of action and development. They can replace a mother or father as a role model and lead a young person to take on beliefs and attitudes not shared by their families. The choice of a later career may depend on such influence. There is nothing inherently wrong in this where the teacher elicits from the child qualities which would otherwise have remained undeveloped. Trouble does arise, however, where a child is torn by greatly conflicting influences from the two sources. Some young people can create something very much their own from whatever experience offers them; others are divided, feeling neither in touch with their origins nor part of a new environment.

The Crucial Event

To many people, one particular event in their early lives is responsible for much of what became of them later. The death of a parent or sibling, separation from the family through evacuation or going into care, the parents' divorce or moving to another country are those most often referred to. There may be vivid memories of the event itself or only assumptions made about its impact which seem to make sense of how the person is now. Although he had only faint memories of being sent away to boarding school at six, Robert was convinced that all his difficulties with relationships and poor self-image sprang from the rejection by his mother that he must have experienced. One-off experiences can also have profound significance. A woman put her longstanding anxiety down to the moment she saw another child run over when she was four. Another saw winning a prize for verse-speaking at the age of seven as transforming her entire sense of herself from a failure to someone who could be worth something.

Such events are not always put forward as the one determining factor in a person's development, of course. But they often seem to symbolise a turning point. Of greater interest than the events themselves is how people see themselves as changing as a result of them. The occurrence may represent loss, deprivation or the stunting of potential growth and achievement. Or it can signal a new and richer phase in a person's life, either through offering fresh opportunities or stirring them to fight against odds with a resilience they did not know they had. Either way, it has contributed much to their construing of themselves.

Having a Handicap

People born with a handicap or developing a disability of some kind early in life may or may not construe it as a central aspect of their personality. Much will depend on its severity but more perhaps on how they are responded to by significant others when they are young. If the focus is placed mainly by the parents and the rest of the family on the fact that the child has difficulty walking or talking or cannot see or hear as others do, the chances of the child's personality evolving around the fact of being handicapped are high. If, on the other hand, he or she is seen as a child first, a particular child, with all the attributes any child has then the disability may take its place as only one factor to be taken into account. It may not be possible to ignore it but it need not govern the child's entire perception of self.

There is no denying that some people's choices in life *are* severely limited. We may look to the examples of the Helen Kellers of this world who seem endowed with some extraordinary power to overcome devastating losses. But there are many for whom such experience is not possible. We can only respect and try to facilitate what they are able to make of their lives. There are instances, however, where limitation may have more to do with the degree to which a less extensive difficulty has been focused on to form the core of a person's self-perception.

One striking example of this can be seen in people who stutter. For some, disfluency may be frustrating, depressing sometimes, but they do not construe themselves solely in terms of their ability to speak. Asked who and what they are they will describe their jobs, where they come from, various roles in life. Ask others about themselves and uppermost in their minds will be the fact that they are "stutterers". It is this fact that has governed their relationships, their choice of work, the interests they have pursued. These people may not stutter severely from the listener's point of view but their fear of disfluency may totally preoccupy them.

Less obviously seen as a handicap but sometimes just as painfully experienced is a person's perception of their size. Many women especially are intensely conscious of being fat and judge themselves and others first and foremost on this "fat vs thin" dimension. The implications for acceptability and worth can be vast. A person may feel forced into the stereotyped behaviours expected of them and never show many aspects of themselves. Their lives too are dominated by this one attribute and many choices made in the light of it.

I made up My Mind

So far the factors we have looked at which can be seen as crucial determinants of personality are, on the whole, those over which people feel they have little control. Something was passed down to them, done to them, happened to them, and although they have sometimes made something good out of it their development was to a certain extent dependent on it. There are those, however, who seem at some point more clearly to choose how they will be entirely for themselves. We hear tell of statesmen, famous sportsmen and women, people who devote their lives to a religion or a specific profession who decide at a particular moment in their lives that this is what they will do and nothing can deflect them from their path. We also come across such people in our daily lives, not destined to fame but who seem to choose more spontaneously. These are the people, too, who can change direction just as clearly and completely. It is as if they are more fully self-creating than the rest of us. And yet we all have something of this capacity in us. We all have moments when we go beyond ourselves—in moments of danger perhaps or intense emotion. At such times something is so important that many of the limitations of our biography, our conditioning, our circumstances are swept aside.

We close this section with a diagram (Figure 3.1) summarising the important elements in personal theories.

In much of what Kelly says about people as experimenters and creators of their own worlds, he is in effect inviting us to extend this capacity of ours to invent ourselves anew and change what we do not like about ourselves. If "all of our present interpretations of the universe are subject to revision or replacement" (1) this must above all include our interpretations

PERSONAL THEORIES

GOVERNING FACTORS	HOW THEY CAN BE CONSTRUED
Heredity (Its in the genes)	—That's how I am —What can I make of my inheritance?
Family, racial, social context (I was born to it)	—This is my path —There are other roads to take
The Influence of Others (It was my mother)	—They made me what I am —I will be different
External happenings (The crucial event)	—The point at which I stopped —The point at which I took off
Internal happenings (Having a handicap)	—These are my limits —There is more to me than that
Self-creation (I made up my mind)	—I am myself —I can change —What shall I become next?

Figure 3.1   Important elements in personal theories

of ourselves. Few of us are courageous enough to leap into the dark and change to something we know nothing of and few of us would be foolish enough to turn ourselves into someone we loathed. But most of us can make some changes if we summon up the energy and imagination.

Look back at what you wrote before reading this section and see whether any of the examples lead you to question the assumptions you have made about factors contributing to the development of your personality. It is not to see whether you "got it right" or got it wrong. It is to reflect whether there are alternative ways of looking at some element in your life which up until now has seemed inevitably a governing influence. If you feel, for example, that an early relationship has limited your choices, held you back, does it need to go on doing so? Can you see some traumatic event in your childhood as past? You don't have to forget it or try to see it as other than it was. But can you leave it behind? We hope that later chapters in this book can help you if you feel that some change in this area would be beneficial.

FORMAL THEORIES OF DEVELOPMENT

We have said that we do not intend to make a comprehensive survey of existing theories of personality development. This is in no way to underestimate their value but simply because this book does not set out to do more than try to convey the essence of personal construct psychology. However, it does seem of interest to consider some of them briefly in the light of perhaps the most important dimension emerging from our outline of personal theories: the sense of freedom or limitation inherent in the views held as to how our personalities are formed and evolve. Although people as a whole do not scour the psychological literature in order to find a specific theory to adopt, psychological approaches are developed within a climate of thought at a particular time and in their turn can influence that climate.

Freedom vs Determinism in Psychological Approaches

In one of the most enlightening and readable books on personality theory, Hjelle and Ziegler (5), discuss a number of basic assumptions about human nature which they see as profoundly influencing "the way that individuals perceive one another, treat one another and, in the case of personality theorists, construct theories about one another". And the first of these, which they express in the form of a bipolar construct, is this crucial question of how free we are to control what happens to us or how much our actions are governed by forces beyond our power to choose or even be aware of. They point out that those who assert that we are potentially self-determining vary in their views as to how we may reach that potential and what can prevent us from doing so. Others presenting our behaviour as determined differ in what they see as the factors governing us. Implicit in the first group is the notion that we are primarily responsible for our own actions and capable of change, while the second group imply that understanding how we come to be as we are is the best we can hope for. They give Carl Rogers as an example of one who places us on the "freedom" side of the construct. He states that "man does not simply have the characteristics of a machine, he is not simply in the grip of unconscious motives, he is a person who creates meaning in life, a person who embodies a dimension of subjective freedom" (6). In contrast, on the "determinism" pole comes B.F. Skinner, who maintains that a person "is completely determined by his conditioning history"..."one does what one is reinforced to do". As they consider a wide range of personality theories, these authors find writers of very different persuasions coming together on the same pole. (This highlights the importance of exploring the personal meaning of the verbal labels given to any construct.)

Freud, for example, they see as equally extreme on the determinism side but for entirely different reasons. To him it is the power of the unconscious which governs us. In his view "all human events (actions, thoughts, feelings, aspirations) are governed by laws and determined by powerful instinctual forces, notably sex and aggression" of which we can never be fully aware. "In such a theoretical system", they say, "there is no room for concepts such as free will, choice, personal responsibility, volition, spontaneity and self-determination". Personality is shaped by early childhood experiences and change in adulthood is extremely difficult if not impossible.

Maslow's humanistic theory joins that of Rogers on the freedom pole but, again, the meaning of that freedom is different. With his emphasis on the person's "needs" and the tendency to seek personal goals which make life meaningful he sees human beings as fundamentally free and responsible for their own behaviour. "This freedom is manifest in whether one decides to satisfy one's needs, how one chooses to satisfy them, and, specifically, how one gropes toward self-actualization. A person *decides* what her or his potentialities are and how she or he will actualize them".

In Figure 3.2 we have adapted the format designed by Hjelle and Ziegler to position their theorists on their nine basic assumptions about human nature and show how a range of approaches compare on this particular dimension.

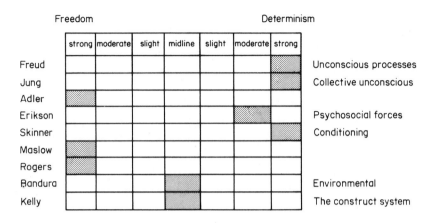

Figure 3.2   Theorists and their assumptions on human nature

A PERSONAL CONSTRUCT VIEW OF DEVELOPMENT

The Freedom and Limitation of the Construing Person

As you see in Figure 3.2, Kelly is placed at the midpoint on this freedom/determinism construct. He views the construct system as providing a person with

> "both freedom of decision and limitation of action— freedom, because it permits him to deal with the meaning of events rather than forces him to be helplessly pushed around by them, and limitation because he can never make choices outside the world of alternatives he has erected for himself." (1).

He in no way denies the influence of "unconscious forces", but chooses to look at them in terms of those aspects of our construing which are preverbal (perhaps developed before we had language) or not currently available at a high level of awareness owing to their irrelevance, the threat they pose or some change in our overall construing of things. He *is* concerned with social and environmental influences but from the point of view of what the individual makes of them, rather than specifying the effects of particular factors. Conditioning plays no part in his view of personal growth and reinforcement is replaced by the very important notion of the part played by validation and invalidation in the formation of our ways of construing. Our construction of something is validated if our predictions of an event are confirmed. It is invalidated if we find we are wrong. (All these ideas will be discussed further in the next chapter.)

The Development of Construing in Children

A number of theories of child development attempt to explain how we come to be as we are in relation to psychosexual "stages" or in terms of intense emotions towards the mother. Others view a child's growth more externally through measurement of abilities, setting various skills against certain "norms" of achievement. All of them may throw light on aspects of how a person comes to be. None of them presents a comprehensive picture of the experience of growing from the inside.

What we are attempting to do here is explore how the complex system of personal constructs which we have called our "personality" might have evolved from the earliest experiences of infants. It is possible to see the development of the embryo in the womb from the moment of conception in terms of aspects of construing. There is movement, change, evidence of response to events both inside and outside the mother's body. But we have chosen to begin at birth with our proposal as to how babies' earliest awareness of themselves and their environment might take the form of the processes of discrimination and prediction which we see more highly developed in older children and adults.

We cannot *know* how babies begin to make sense of themselves and the world around them. Few of us can remember how things were at a very early age and observation of an infant's behaviour can only lead us to guess what he or she might be experiencing. But of one thing we can be sure: the youngest child is active from the beginning and there is no reason to doubt that what we observe is part of an effort to find some meaning in what is going on inside and around them. They have no language to help to clarify the confusion of feelings, sensations, sounds, visual impressions, so we can only try to suspend our more sophisticated trappings and tune into those processes which were all we had when we began.

A baby lying awake in a cot has a limited range of vision, little discrimination for the various sounds in the room or outside. Bodily sensations are probably her most vivid kinds of experience. So how might she be "construing"? When she is warm and comfortable her body is more relaxed but will immediately respond in contrasting tension to being damp or cold. Hunger will signal itself as pain inside, while satisfaction after food will feel completely different. There is a need to be held, enfolded, which most mothers respond to. It is hard to put into words the state which brings this need about but it must be something to do with the feeling of being "lost", "alone", "isolated". It could be argued that these are universal experiences which just "happen" and the baby is simply responding to changing "stimuli". But they can be seen as some of the earliest constructs a baby develops. And they remain throughout life, with others, as fundamental aspects of a person's being.

As we grow, warmth and coldness take on meaning beyond that physical comfort or discomfort. Hunger and satisfaction can embrace all kinds of powerful wishes and their fulfilment. Being in touch with the world or isolated can apply to many aspects of life. And for each one of us the implications will be different. This in itself suggests that we have made something personal of the original experiences. In a later chapter we shall be looking at ways of exploring the personal meaning of "core" constructs such as these and it may be interesting for you to try to trace the development of your own.

At another level, it is clear from an infant's reactions that some textures are pleasant to touch and others unpleasant, that some sounds fix their attention while others are ignored. It is highly likely that smells are very significant, human as well as nonhuman, and the smell of mother and the taste of her must soon become distinct from all that is "not-mother". Just when one voice becomes known and distinguished from others or a face recognised from among other faces probably varies from child to child, but we can observe differences in response towards those who care for them and those who are strangers from quite early on.

Children who are limited in movement, vision, hearing or any other aspect of their being may clearly be prevented from making some of these early discriminations. Those who cannot reach out to touch or grasp things will lack those dimensions of shape and texture which are such an important part of our beginning to understand the nature of things. People who care for them learn to help them hold things in their hands, place them against their skin to give them something of this experience. A child who cannot see is encouraged from the beginning to touch and hold, a child who cannot hear to watch and feel any vibrations with their hands from an object, a person's throat, a cat's body when it purrs. One young boy who had been deaf from birth described people as "shouting" or "speaking quietly" from the movement of their faces and would flinch at the former as surely as a hearing child.

Just as those early, fundamental experiences were seen to be actively construed by the infant so the young baby comes to know something of the world through movement and the senses and it is clear that very soon they come to make something of the outcomes of their own behaviour. Random actions are repeated and come to have a stable meaning—the movement of something hanging on the cot, the sensation produced by positions of their bodies, the feeling of their lips when they blow repeatedly or suck. More importantly, the infant begins to elicit responses from the people around her and gradually learns to "predict" them. These are as much experiments as more sophisticated behaviour and go towards making sense of their personal worlds. The range of emotions aroused in them in the course of these activities shows us the *total* involvement that is the experience of construing. Out of awareness, then, and action, children gradually develop some notions of how things and people are and, above all, begin to learn about themselves.

These discoveries form the basis of a system of constructs which in older people we are able to explore directly through asking how they see things.

Relating to Others

Almost all theories emphasise the importance of the relationship between mothers and their children. It is generally agreed that it is here that the main foundations are laid for later relationships. But the stress seems always to be on how mothers respond to their children, the effects of loving care or inadequate nurturing. It is as if the child is the passive recipient of all that is done to them and only able to react with anger or despair if things go wrong or flourish if all goes well. A personal construct approach, however, sees the development of the relationship as reciprocal. It is the interplay between the two which a number of writers have considered. As we have said, young children are construing those around them from very early on. They change as they understand something from the outcomes of their own behaviour. The mothers, too, are trying to find meaning in their infants' behaviour. Both are changing as a result. Joy O'Reilly (7) reminds us that giving birth to a baby, learning to live with a growing being may give a woman a great deal of new information about herself, demanding enormous adaptation of her, just as babies discover much about themselves through her.

Great emphasis has been placed on the trauma experienced by children who are neglected by their parents or deprived of the affection and warmth we all need. But mothers, too, need response to their caring and their sense of worth can be seriously undermined if this is not shown. In the field of autism, at one time, the mother's lack of response to her child was regarded as the cause of the infant's withdrawal. Now more attention is paid to the effect on a caring mother of her child's lack of response to *her*. Such a mother will, like all mothers, have expectations of how it will be between herself and her baby. If these are not realised, her guilt as to her own fulfilment of her role will be shattering.

In normal circumstances, however, the relationship between mother and child develops through a process of gradually coming to give meaning to each other's behaviour and, as we have said, the child is as active in this as the parent. Bannister and Fransella (8) see the child's construing of the mother's construct system as the "jumping off ground for the development of its own construing system". Through her the infant "starts to single out aspects of the environment as distinct from the pair of them, and later to single out its mother as different from others, and eventually to single out itself as different from her". It should be stressed, though, that while the child looks to the mother to help make sense of things it is his or her own interpretation of what the mother means by her behaviour and, later, what she says, that will go to form the basis of his or her own construing. Particularly when a child begins to use the language of adults we too readily assume that they mean what we mean, so even here it will be personal and individual.

Nevertheless, if we are careful to bear that in mind, as children acquire language it does become possible to understand something of both the focus of their construing and the ways in which they may set about the process. And such development continues to evolve from a combination of their own personal experiments and what they understand of the construing of others. As a young child plays alone it will be discovering both the possibilities of the objects around it and its own possibilities in terms of manipulation, strength, balance and so on. As it plays with others, it needs to observe, and listen to what they are doing or saying in order to take part in a game or activity which has some kind of joint purpose. Constructs to do with being in control of things or people or being frustrated by them begin early and both the child's own persistence and others' facilitation or lack of it will be important factors in this aspect of its growth. Validation at every level, from interest in what they do and encouragement to a sense of being wanted, loved, included, is crucial to a later sense of worth.

Clearly, however important the child's relationship with the mother, growth will also depend on interaction with others. Just as it takes on what it understands of mother's meanings, so it is influenced by other members of the family, other children it plays with, teachers when it goes to school. Such varied relationship is important to allow a child to modify the perceptions of just one person in the light of other views. Through them its attention is drawn to a wider range of possibilities and its choices are greater. Where this opportunity is lacking, a child will be more limited in its own experiments and may only have the option to conform or contradict. Our observation of young people's preoccupations match with the findings of studies concerned with the nature of the constructs they are able to put into words. Just as young children explore and are absorbed by the physical aspects of things and people so they are found around the age of seven years, say, to describe people largely in terms of their appearance and what they do:

"bigger than me vs small"
"fights a lot vs doesn't fight"
"shouts at people vs doesn't shout"
"clever at making things vs doesn't make things"
"rushes about all the time vs sits still"
"has long hair vs has short hair"

Such "psychological;' constructs as this child used were much less specific and more comprehensive:

"nice vs nasty"
"happy vs sad"
"naughty vs never naughty"

By ten years, when children tend to be more concerned with relationships, especially with their peers, Brierly (9) found that they were using more constructs descriptive of personality such as these from a girl of this age:

"boring vs nice to play with"
"frightened of things vs not frightened"
"kind vs mean"
"clever vs stupid"

By thirteen, he found that such descriptions and references to behaviour predominated, as here:

"sporting, active vs lazy"
"even-tempered vs hot-tempered"

"tries to make a fool of people vs doesn't tease people"
"conscientious vs doesn't work"

This small sample in itself suggests the world of school, where sport, schoolwork and friendships are often of major importance. Since we know that children of different backgrounds and different races have different preoccupations, it is a pity that there is so little in the literature showing the kinds of constructs used by them. A child from a rural setting or who works from a very young age to help maintain the family will undoubtedly focus on these activities and what is significant about the experiences for them. It would help us to understand what life is like for a young person living in poverty on the streets of Delhi if we knew their important themes and issues. Of equal interest would be to know whether children from other cultures also have different *ways* of construing.

Some attempts have been made to discover how the construct systems of Western children might develop in terms of organisation. Phillida Salmon (10) suggests that very young children differ from older ones not only in the smaller number of constructs available to them but also in these being less organised. This allows them to change their view more easily as new experiences challenge their expectations. Bannister and Fransella (8) survey the various studies and conclude that although this question of organisation is not clearly answered, younger children seem to see things in more black and white terms while as children grow older they are able to discriminate between people more, use a wider ranger of constructs, as we would expect, and more "shades of grey". The system becomes more complex and differences emerge between boys and girls, with the former's greater preoccupation with activities and abilities and the latter's with interpersonal relationships.

We shall say more of tight and loose construing but we can see how a strong tendency towards one or the other may show itself very early on. Salmon describes the rigid child whose behaviour is entirely rule-bound and who cannot cope with exceptions to these rules. They "lose their spontaneity of thought and feeling all too early in life". And in contrast there are those who "fail ever to come to grips with reality, and wander through their adult years with childish non-comprehension". When we meet these people in adulthood, especially in therapy, their construing is certainly found to be over-organised on the one hand and lacking in structure on the other. The "problem" lies as much in this aspect of their approach to life as in the content of the troubles they bring. How we function in terms of our construing and what can go wrong will be discussed fully in the next two chapters.

How we Come to Know Ourselves

We have already touched on a number of aspects of children's developing view of the self: the effects of the behaviour of others towards them, the outcomes of early experiments of their own. And we must stress again that what we are concerned with is the child's own view which results from these experiences, not some kind of external suppositions or measurements. A major process involved in making sense of all this in relation to discovering who we are is the discrimination between the "self" and "others" which Kelly proposed and Bannister and Fransella found borne out by results of various studies. Babies, as we have said, learn to distinguish between themselves and their mothers. If there are other children in the family it is likely that they themselves notice ways in which they and their brothers and sisters are similar or different, as well as hearing from their parents the distinctions between them that we noted before. As their world widens, they have more opportunities for comparison and contrast and so we can see how this may form the basis of a child's self-image.

We cannot ask young children to tell us directly what sort of person they are but we can gain a tentative impression of this from observing their behaviour. A four-year-old who enters a new situation with a beaming smile and moves about the room freely inspecting what is there seems to have expectations of being accepted and welcome. He is "being" the kinds of attributes older people will spell out about themselves: "confident", "relaxed", "not shy". One who hangs back and looks for a reaction whenever she touches anything must have reason to doubt herself. Perhaps she is the sort of person who "gets things wrong". The former turned out to be much loved by his parents and grandparents, the latter was continually criticised for untidiness or clumsiness by the mother, who described her older sister as "no problem at all".

Young children's self-statements are worth noting. They are often in terms of what they can or cannot *do* in comparison with others: "I can carry all this by myself. Lucy's too small". "I wish I could stay up after tea to watch television like Danny. It's not fair." Or what they possess: "I've got six cars, he's only got four". "Our Christmas tree is much bigger than yours." Or (sadly) "Maureen's got a mummy *and* a daddy." Trivial as all but the last of these comparisons may seem to us as adults, they probably represent important issues for the children themselves and show us clearly that this process goes on at an everyday level at least. Most of us can reflect on our own childhoods, where our achievements in contrast to others' or an opportunity, attribute or possession they had and we did not, was of intense concern.

Underlining this "self versus others" discrimination in the development of our view of ourselves is the fact that we make judgements about others in relation to what is important for us. For the child who described people as "fighting a lot" as opposed to "not fighting", physical aggression was an important means of relating to others. Children do not normally consider how people speak, but a child who stutters will often produce constructs such as "talks well ... can't talk", when asked to say something about those he or she knows. Just as we found that someone concerned about her weight will look at others first in relation to "fat vs thin". Since our view of ourselves is part of our construct system as a whole, how we see ourselves will be reflected in our stance towards the world. If we develop a poor self-image, we are likely to approach life in a fairly pessimistic way.

Personality as a Process of Change

We have attempted in this chapter to look at our development as people in the light of what we make of events, our relationships with others and our perceptions of ourselves. It should be clear that a personal construct view of how we come to be as we are is concerned with an ongoing process. Our construing of certain basic experiences will of course have a profound effect on our anticipations of what is to come. We shall see from later chapters that it is hard and can be very threatening to challenge assumptions which have governed our ways of dealing with things.

Nevertheless, it is Kelly's belief that

"there are always some alternative constructions available to choose among in dealing with the world. No one needs to paint himself into a corner; no one needs to be completely hemmed in by circumstances; no one needs to be the victim of his biography." (1)

In theory, then, we can all change and we go on changing all our lives. Most of us can pinpoint moments when we were aware of something new entering our experience; a quite different relationship, a new environment, some fresh field of activity or an added responsibility. We know then that we are "adapting", looking at things in a new light. This can be exciting and enhancing. At other times we may realise that something different is demanded of us but feel unable to make sense of new events and the feelings they arouse in us. Life is threatening. We may try to maintain the status quo by shutting out all that is difficult to deal with or sink into helpless confusion. Alternatively, we may call upon that ability to meet something new with an attitude of enquiry which we found in the infant playing in the cot. Whatever we do, whatever choice we make, will be part of the continuing process of becoming who we are.

4

HOW DO WE WORK?

There is a large element of the ridiculous in having a single chapter entitled 'How do we work'. Human beings are exceedingly complex entities generally, and from the psychological perspective especially. Whatever else this chapter is going to achieve it can only be a snapshot of all the processes going on to a greater or lesser extent in one individual. Indeed, in order to present some of these processes, it is necessary to describe them separately, as though they were discrete entities. As you progress through this chapter, being introduced to new ideas and constructs, try to remember that in a person they are all working continuously in time, changing and altering and interacting amongst themselves, in a perpetual state of motion and flux.

There is one further issue to address before moving into specifics. That is that PCP does not go along with the traditional psychological trilogy of emotion, cognition and conation. Kelly (2) in his essay on "The psychotherapeutic relationship" tells how the theory has been described as cognitive, emotional, existentialist; to do with dialectical materialism, learning theory and Zen Buddhism; behaviourist and psychoanalytic.

One of the reasons for such a range of descriptions which encompass almost all the psychological possibilities, is that PCP simply does not recognise the distinctions most other approaches are based upon. Although much of what we discuss about PCP is verbal, this does not make it a cognitive theory. It is only verbal to the extent that, being abstract, words are used to try to communicate the issues as clearly as possible. And when it comes to working with clients, words are usually the first medium of communication.

People often say that PCP is a "cold" theory; that somehow emotion is excluded, and that everything is reduced to rather mechanistic explanations. This is not true, although it is understandable that people can believe it. The fact that the theory is couched in such abstract terms makes it appear rarefied and distanced from everyday emotion and being. But it is only abstract in the sense that it covers *all* aspects of psychological functioning, and in order to explain that it has to be presented fairly abstractly. PCP defines *everything* as a form of construing. At its most accessible, thinking is clearly construing. We can immediately understand the verbal labels of the constructs and their contrast poles. Behaviour is slightly harder to understand as construing, but in terms of behaviour being itself an experiment in its own right, it can be assimilated fairly easily. But emotion is much harder to explain as a form of construing. You can hear words, and see behaviour, and so both of these are relatively easily communicated from one person to another. But emotion is about what you *feel*, and this is much more personal and private.

Various people have attempted to explore the field of emotion within PCP. Kelly himself described such states as anxiety, guilt and aggressiveness (see below) without fully exploring the emotional minefield. Mildred McCoy (11) developed the field rather further by attempting to translate many emotional experiences into PCP terminology to show the process occurring at the time. Herein lies the major difficulty. Because emotions are so personal and so private, and often so overwhelming, many people find it almost incomprehensible to think of them as a psychological process in their own right, and still less as operating by the same principles as other psychological processes. Yet this is exactly what PCP says.

The idea that all three traditionally separated psychological functions are in fact unified with the same set of psychological processes is one of the hardest parts of PCP to grasp hold of, yet it is absolutely essential. We work holistically, not as a collection of discrete processes operating by different laws. It may be a difficult concept to grasp, but it is also very attractive. Most people would rather, we suspect, be regarded a whole beings than a collection of ill-fitting, overlapping processes, apparently at war with each other at best, or simply ignorant of each other. This totality of function, together with the notion of perpetual motion, of processes always in action, underpins the PCP idea of how we all work. Whatever individual constructs we present below, these principles should always be borne in mind.

One word of caution as we progress into a Kellyan view of how we work: many theories invent their own terminology for whatever processes they are describing. Others use common words without defining them clearly, assuming that there is a commonality of meaning amongst readers or practitioners. Kelly actually does neither of these but takes up a third option. He uses words as labels for constructs and processes, many of which—such as anxiety, aggressiveness, hostility—appear very familiar, and he then defines them precisely in PCP terms. What often happens as a result is that the word retains contact with its common meaning, but is redefined subtly either to broaden the concept, or to lose some commonly held prejudicial associations. To give one example here, aggressiveness tends to be something in general terms people view rather negatively. It tends to be associated with violence to someone, or the effects of force on someone else. Indeed it is defined by how someone else sees a person acting, not by what process is occurring within the person displaying the aggressiveness. Kelly *always* defines his terms on what is happening within the person, *not* how someone else experiences this. Thus in this example, aggressiveness is the "active elaboration of one's perceptual field". As such, it is quite a positive thing to be doing. And there are a whole variety of ways in which such active elaboration could take place, *including* being aggressive in the more traditional sense.

LEVELS OF COGNITIVE AWARENESS

If we start with more general issues relating to how we work, then Kelly's approach to the old divisions between the unconscious, subconscious and conscious need to be mentioned. Kelly obviously does not subscribe to the analytic view of there being an unconscious under the influence of a maelstrom of drives and desires, ultimately affecting the way the individual reacts and behaves. The only force, or drive, he acknowledges is that of trying to make sense of the world about you, with the curiosity and "man-the-scientist" activity that this engenders.

However, it is clear that no individual is aware of all his construing processes all the time. Indeed, as individuals, we are probably only aware of a very small minority at any time. These are the constructs for which we have provided suitable labels in order to be able to think about them, or communicate about them. In other words, we are cognitively aware of them. These are constructs at a high level of cognitive awareness. A construct at a low level of cognitive awareness is one which is used without any clear labels, and, indeed, exists without you being aware of its action. This equates in part to the notion of the "unconscious" but without all the dynamic components some other theories would invest in it.

Of course, constructs can be raised from a low to a high level of cognitive awareness, such as in therapy. One of the purposes of exploring one's construct system, either with someone else or on one's own, is precisely to bring up to a high level of cognitive awareness some of the constructs which you have been using, but which may have been causing you some difficulties without your being aware whence the difficulty stemmed.

In order to try and help you find your way through the basics of how we work, we have divided the remainder of this chapter into two parts—types of constructs, and processes in the construct system. To some extent such a division is arbitrary, especially since some of the types of constructs, or descriptions of them, also relate to the processes they may get involved with. Such a division, made purely for the purposes of instruction and introduction, should therefore not be regarded as anything other than a useful *aide-memoire*. The processes use the constructs, and different kinds of constructs change how the processes work. As PCP states, we, as people are in perpetual psychological motion, and thus the description which follows can be likened to a series of black and white photographs of what is going on. It will give you a lot of information, but not necessarily a sense of movement. You have to keep that in mind yourself.

TYPES OF CONSTRUCTS

1. Preverbal, Non-verbal and Verbal Constructs

To some extent this may appear to overlap with our discussion of levels of cognitive awareness above, but in fact, they are dealing with different issues. High-level constructs are by definition verbal because they have labels and can be thought about, and communicated socially. Low-level constructs are generally non-verbal but may be verbalisable—as they are discovered in therapy for example. Preverbal constructs are those developed before speech occurred and are deep-seated constructs acquired from the very earliest experiments carried out as a baby, and are usually connected to love, warmth, feeding and so forth.

As Kelly writes about preverbal constructs (1):

> "In dealing with a preverbal construct it is important to realize that, ordinarily, it is one which was originally designed to construe those elements of which an infant could be aware. One should therefore not expect his adult client to describe or portray a preverbal construct in a manner which is becoming to a mature person. The therapist has before him an infant who is speaking with the voice of an adult."

For many people, such preverbal constructs are incorporated into the construct system as it develops during childhood, adolescence and adulthood, and may cause no difficulties at all. For others, the negative experiences from that time may remain with us, causing increasing difficulties, especially in relationships, without our being able to get hold of exactly what is happening. Clearly the experiments we carry out as infants are few but very important; the results of these are also likely to be fundamental in the basis of our future construct system as a whole. As Kelly points out, though, they are very difficult to talk about, and may in fact form the basis of some important emotions, an area notoriously difficult to talk about rationally.

2. Core Constructs and Peripheral Constructs

These are defined as follows (1):

> "A core construct is one which governs the person's maintenance process."

> "A peripheral construct is one which can be altered without serious modification to the core structure."

Core constructs are essentially those constructs which people use to maintain their identity and existence. They are the constructs which are to do with the definition of *you* on one hand, and the practical needs *you* have in order to continue to exist on the other. These are obviously rather important constructs to any individual. They are often fairly comprehensive constructs, allowing a person to see "a wide variety of known events as consistent with his own personality" (1). Within the core structure as a whole are core role constructs which relate to interactions between yourself and others, and yourself and society. This was initially discussed in Chapter 2 in relation to the sociality corollary. How you see your own role in relation to others is clearly very important to you, and your maintenance of a social identity. Thus core constructs are of various kinds, and are extremely vital. They are central in your view of yourself, both personally and in relation to your social circumstances.

Peripheral constructs, being defined as they are effectively as being non-core constructs, are more to do with general events or activities. They can be changed or altered much more easily, usually with little or no immediate effect on your own identity or role.

Later in this chapter, we will be discussing constructs of transition, but it should be mentioned briefly here that enforced change of core constructs tends to produce *threat*, while somehow ending up behaving contrary to your normal expectation of your role (as defined by your core role constructs) produces *guilt*.

3. Propositional, Pre-emptive and Constellatory Constructs

These three descriptive labels for types of construct relate more to how you use them, than to what part of the system they inhabit. Propositional constructs are those you use to try on for size in a situation which you are trying to explain to yourself. This situation may be X, so let us treat it *as if* it were X. Construct X does not therefore force you to consider the situation as anything other than the possibility that it might be X. Propositional constructs are our most useful method of encountering and incorporating new elements into our construct system.

A pre-emptive construct, by contrast, is one which, when applied, demands that you see the element it is applied to as described by that construct and *only* that. For example, a ball is a ball and only a ball, it cannot be considered as a leather object, or a door-stop or whatever else. The construct refuses to allow any other construction of the element save that provided by the pre-emptive construct. Many of our prejudices are based upon pre-emptive constructs, and they can be very difficult to shift.

A constellatory construct, as its name implies, is one which carries with it a constellation of other constructs on the principle that if one applies, then they all apply. Once you have used the constellatory construct, then you are lumbered with the whole package. The ball, mentioned above, may for example also be defined as round, dangerous, break windows and be childish. Whenever this person sees something he or she construes as a ball, all these other constructs automatically come along for the ride. Obviously this can make for rather rigid construing, and cause endless difficulties in communication with another person who is perhaps being propositional about the same object or event.

4. Regnant Constructs

A regnant construct is defined as "a kind of superordinate construct which assigns each of its elements to a category on an all-or-none basis". It can be seen as a special kind of pre-emptive construct at a high level of abstraction which may govern a person's attitude to a whole aspect of life. In some ways it simplifies things, leaving no room for argument. Some people's view of sex roles, for example, may be governed by regnant constructs. A man is seen as "the provider", perhaps. Subordinate implications may be that he works hard, is strong, unemotional and the head of the household. There is no room for doubt in this which would allow a man not to work, to shed a tear occasionally and perhaps concede to his wife from time to time. Equally, there is no question that a woman might fulfil this role. There may be evidence that such things occur, but the people involved are not truly "men" or "women" in the proper sense!

5. Tight and Loose Constructs

"Tight constructs are those which lead to unvarying predictions." (1)

while loose constructs

"are those which lead to varying predictions but which, for practical purposes, may be said to retain their identities." (1)

This loose–tight dimension is a valuable and much used one. A "tight" construer is someone whose view of life is organised rigidly, full of regular habits, and fast held views on the world. Because his constructs are tight, he makes the same predictions endlessly, without trying out anything new. It is a little like the syndrome of "I like what I know, and I know what I like". A loose construer by contrast seems to make different predictions at the drop of a hat. Other people find them very difficult to predict or subsume simply because their constructs do lead to varying predictions.

In general terms, having either too tight a construct system or too loose a one is likely to cause problems. At the extreme ends of the polarity we might see highly obsessional behaviour at one, while schizophrenic thought disorder has been related to loose construing and is therefore at the other. Most of us, however, lie with a mixture somewhere in between. Our core constructs tend to be tighter, while our peripheral ones are looser; but the precise mix and match depends on the individual concerned.

Tightness and looseness is not, of course, a static state of affairs. Constructs can vary though the spectrum in order to achieve particular objectives. A tight construct is very useful for conducting practical experiments to check out its prediction, while trying to conduct effective experiments with loose constructs is almost impossible and leads to total confusion. Loose constructs, by contrast, are useful propositionally, for trying something out on a new element or a new situation. We all move some of our constructs from tight to loose and back again, conducting an experiment, trying something else out, and then tightening again to conduct a new experiment with the new prediction derived from the loose phase of the cycle. This process, further described below, is called the "creativity cycle".

6. Constructs of Transition

These constructs lie somewhere between being descriptive constructs like those above, and processes such as those we are going on to describe below. They describe what happens to your construct system when put under some pressure either to change or to see yourself as different to the way you have seen yourself up to that point. This is why they are called constructs of *transition*, because they tend to be about transition and movement, often unpleasant. They should be differentiated from the process of validation and invalidation which is the continuing process of outcome from experiments going on under your control, and which lead to change in the system as new constructs are incorporated and old ones discarded, or suspended.

(a) Threat

> "threat is the awareness of an imminent comprehensive change in one's core structures." (1)

Clearly this is a major event. As we have seen above, our core structures are about our identity and its maintenance. An imminent comprehensive change is a fairly drastic assault on the very centre of our being. And being aware of such an imminent trauma leads to threat. We don't want such a thing to happen (usually) and therefore the response to threat is either to try and avoid the change, or to try to make it not happen in a certain way. We can all think of times when we feel that we have been threatened in such a way: we may consider ourselves clear and helpful writers, and this may be integral to our core views of ourselves, so if a collection of reviewers describe our writing as obscure and impossible to understand, we may well feel under threat. Of course, we can accept their judgement, and reorganise our core constructs accordingly (and indeed, if such experiences continue this is exactly what we should do). Alternatively, if our original view is very important to our idea of ourselves say professionally, then we may choose to find ways of discounting what the critics have written. Perhaps they have not really read our writing properly, or they were not capable of understanding it, or all reviewers are jerks, or we may even refuse to read any criticism at all. In each of these scenarios, we are attempting to defuse the threat posed by these nasty reviewers, and we may well succeed, at least in the short term.

Threat feels extremely uncomfortable, and may be associated with the physiological sensations connected with outrage or panic. It may tend to produce the "fight or flight" kind of reaction, physically as well as psychologically.

(b) Fear

This is the awareness of an imminent incidental change in one's core structure. Clearly this could still be fairly unpleasant, but it is not so drastic as threat. The degree of potential change to one's core structures is what differentiates threat from fear, although some of the reactions to it may be very similar.

(c) Anxiety

Kelly defines this as:

> "the awareness that the events with which one is confronted lie outside the range of convenience of his construct system." (1)

Put simply, the person does not know what to do. He is faced with an event or set of events for which his construct system is quite unprepared. Hence anxiety develops. How he goes about dealing with this anxiety of course depends upon the structure he has. If it is a very tight structure (cf. "tight" above) he may find it extremely difficult to do anything, and will merely keep trying to apply his current constructs in the hope that something will work. Conversely, someone with a more flexible system may be able to take current constructs and see if they can be adapted to deal with what is being faced. He may creatively move between tightness and looseness to try and develop some understanding, and thereby extend the range of convenience of the system.

(d) Guilt

This is the

> "awareness of dislodgment of the self from one's core role structure." (1)

Fairly obviously, this is what happens when you do something that you normally don't see yourself as doing. Perhaps you think you are a quiet and tolerant person, and you have just yelled at your secretary over something trivial. If being quiet and tolerant is important to your perception of yourself—that is to say is part of your core role structure—then this change of behaviour will act as a "dislodgment from your core role structure" and you will feel guilt as a result.

If you have the kind of core role structure which says "anything goes" or you have no particular fixed ideas about what kind of person you are, or what beliefs are important to you, then guilt is unlikely to worry you particularly. This might be a description of the psychopathic personality, where whatever that person does is acceptable to him, so long as he construes it as being in his interests!

Guilt can be very damaging to an individual, and, if the precipitating event is serious enough, can become quite debilitating psychologically. For any individual, what is serious may be vastly different, and even an apparently trivial issue to one person may be of such core role import to another as to produce a huge guilt reaction. Where the dislodgement is major, the person may end up "consumed by guilt", still hanging on to their original perception of themselves, but unable to deal with the evidence that that is not how they actually behaved. A soldier, fit and strong, going into battle, who then avoids a situation in which he might have been killed but has resulted in a mate being killed or injured, might be in such a position. He has always seen himself as one who would rush in regardless of personal safety, but when the crunch came, he discovered he did not, with terrible consequences.

(e) Hostility

This is

> "the continued effort to extort validational evidence in favour of a type of social prediction which has already been recognised as a failure." (1)

In this situation, the individual tries out a social prediction, conducts the experiment and gets the result. So far, so good. But the result is not the one which was wanted, so rather than incorporate that evidence into the original hypothesis, leading to its appropriate amendment, you try to cook the books. Somehow you try to make the experiment give you the result you want. This may involve some manipulation of events or people (who may themselves become aware of what is going on, and resent it even without being able to do anything about it).

A man trying to ask a particular girl to have dinner with him does not wish to accept that she does not want to. Instead of going away and finding another, more amenable girlfriend, he persists by offering increasingly lavish inducements—dinner at an exclusive restaurant, endless flowers and chocolates, repeated telephone calls. The theme remains "you must really want to come out with me." Eventually (and mistakenly) she thinks that she will go out with him once in order to keep him quiet. His hostility has now worked, because although she does not like him any more than she did previously (and probably if he has been very persistent, rather less!), he has managed to force her to go out with him, and has therefore finally validated his social prediction of being the kind of man that all women fall for!

All of us are hostile on some occasions, but usually we learn our lesson fairly fast and accept the results of our experimentation. It is when hostility continues and the attempts to extort the evidence become more and more drastic that major problems occur. And these major problems may not just be within the individual's psychological system, but will be being experienced wherever the extortion is being directed.

(f) Emotional constructs

The four constructs described above, threat, fear, guilt and hostility are ways of describing important emotional events within the terms of PCP. Mildred McCoy (11) proposed a whole range of new professional constructs for various other emotions. She explains that by looking at the four originals it is clear that there is always an element of awareness of the fate or potential fate for some part of the construct system, and various other dimensions including validation vs invalidation, comprehensive vs incidental core structure change, outside vs within the range of convenience of the system, and dislodgement. Using these principles, she proposes new explanations for such emotions as bewilderment (awareness of imminent comprehensive change in non-core structure), love (awareness of validation of one's core structure) and shame (awareness of dislodgement of the self from another's construing of your role).

We have not attempted to present all of them here, or discuss them in any detail. Some people find these descriptions of emotional events cold and distant, and nothing like the event itself. After all, you are hardly likely to lean over a candlelit table and murmur to your partner "you validate my core role constructs, darling". The fact that we can develop within PCP psychological explanations of what appears to be happening which are consistent with the rest of the theory is important both for professional communication and for incorporating emotional experience into the theory itself. But it does not negate the personal experience of that emotion which is an entity in itself, and not usually verbalised.

All of the above constructs, it must be remembered, are not exclusive. Although they have been presented individually, they may and indeed do occur together. A propositional construct may be tight or loose, a regnant construct may be in core structure or in the periphery. Once you have decided a construct is one thing, do not assume it is nothing else as well.

PROCESSES IN THE CONSTRUCT SYSTEM

We have already stated that the division between types of constructs and processes in the system is rather arbitrary. You will discover in what follows many of the constructs you have just met. You may find it necessary to go back and remind yourself of what exactly they were or what they do or describe. It will take you some time to feel at home with all of them, but while on one hand we have often deliberately repeated ourselves to help you, we have not done so every time. This has been partly to conserve space, and partly because we did not wish to underestimate your abilities by assuming you always needed it. Perhaps this is another of our experiments as authors.

1. Dilation and Constriction

Dilation occurs when a person broadens his perceptual field in order to reorganise it on a more comprehensive level. For example, in a field of flowers, a person may start off simply examining one flower in some detail, looking at its petals, stamen and so forth. But in order to consider the context of this flower, he will need to dilate to encompass the field or the area around about. This allows him, but does not require him, to be able to reorganise his constructs of flowers and fields on a more comprehensive level.

Constriction, by contrast, occurs when a person narrows his perceptual field in order to minimise apparent incompatibilities. Here the number of events considered is progressively reduced in order to prevent uncertainty and confusion. Ultimately, such constriction can lead to only one choice being left, that of life or death, so the final constriction is to lead to suicide. However, this is the extreme position and fortunately not usually reached.

It is possible to make a choice between various courses of action by constricting down until only one possibility remains to be considered. This produces rather a blinkered type of approach, whereby when asked why a particular choice has been made, the individual will reply in all honesty that it was the only option. It has become the only option because he has constricted to the extent to make it the only option. Choices are more normally made by use of the CPC cycle (see below).

2. The CPC Cycle

This has to do principally with the usual way of making choices. CPC stands for circumspection, pre-emption and control. Gavin Dunnett has written elsewhere in greater depth on this subject (12). Circumspection is the point at which you consider all the possibilities from amongst the range of constructs at your disposal. The second stage in the cycle is to pre-empt, that is, to come down to only one set of alternatives out of all the ones circumspected around. This is the either–or position. Control comes when you choose which one to act upon, which end of the pre-empted dichotomy upon which to base your experiment.

For example, say you have to travel from London to Aberdeen in Scotland. You have to decide how to get there. The first stage is circumspection. What alternatives do you have? Quite a few, really. You could walk, bicycle, drive your own car, go by motorail or train, fly, try to hitch a lift and so forth. Considering all these is circumspection. Eventually, the second stage, pre-emption is reached. Here you have eliminated all the possibilities to reach either *going by train* vs *not going at all*. Control is the point at which you take the train option. This precipitates you into certain further actions, such as checking the timetables, buying your ticket etc. But you have considered all the options, made a choice and taken control in order to set up the necessary actions.

The area of choice is obviously very important, and one which often causes people great difficulty. This is often, although not always, due to problems with the CPC cycle. One of the most frequent problems is that of impulsivity which is a characteristic foreshortening of the CPC cycle. Almost before the person has time to consider any circumspection, they have moved to pre-empt the issue and take control. He now finds himself committed to his choice despite the fact that he has leapt in with both feet.

Conversely, some people get stuck in the circumspection phase, endlessly considering all the possibilities, and unable to pre-empt. In the example above about the travelling, such a person could say that the advantages of travelling by train would be comfort, but flying would be faster while driving would be more convenient, but then train would be cheaper and so on. Every time he gets near to being able to pre-empt, he slides back into circumspection, often asking all around for advice for good measure.

Problems in the CPC cycle, and with the process of making choices, are often central in working with clients in a PCP way. It is a fascinating area, full of complications and potential problems far beyond our scope to outline here. It links, of course, with the choice corollary whereby choices are made either to extend or consolidate construct systems. The CPC cycle is about how those choices are usually made.

3. The Creativity Cycle

We have already mentioned this when we discussed loose and tight constructs. Creativity implies making something new, usually out of what existed before. This is exactly the process which occurs in the creativity cycle. It starts with loosened construing, where constructs are applied with varying predictions, and ends with tightened and validated construction. This process has something in common with Edward de Bono's ideas of lateral thinking. In this parallel, the lateral thinking is allowing yourself to look at the situation under review from a number of different angles, some of which are not normally applied to this situation. Eventually, you decide that a particular way of approaching it may be worth testing out, and the construct is tightened and an experiment carried out, which hopefully results in validation for the prediction. If, of course, invalidation occurs, the cycle will recur until effective, tight and validated construction has been achieved.

An example comes from a lecturer. She had very tight constructs about lecturing which included the preparation, scientific basis of presentation, non-personal nature of the content, and various other constructs. She was then asked to participate in an informal series of lectures in which she was particularly asked not to be "academic", which was itself the superordinate construct to those already mentioned above. She had to consider various new ways of presenting her material including the use of humour, being more personal, and dressing more informally. She then wrote the lecture based on some of these ideas and its presentation became her experiment, fortunately validated. By loosening her construing to consider alternative predictions, she was able to eventually tighten up and try something different which worked.

It is often thought that only some people are "creative" but the PCP process of creativity is one which we all have and are involved with, whether it be the cook who just comes up with a new dish because he fancied trying different herbs, or the composer who comes up with a new set of sounds. We are all continuously being creative about our own lives.

4. Aggressiveness

We have already defined aggressiveness and made the point that in the PCP definition, it is a positive attribute and one to be encouraged. Each of us is trying to make sense of new events all the time, and the active elaboration of our systems is one way of reducing the possibility of threat and anxiety.

5. Dependency

Most societies nowadays seem to have a common construct of *dependence* vs *independence* in which independence is considered to be the desired pole. Yet PCP argues that dependence is both necessary and desirable. Although the psychological approach is based upon the individual, and what is going on within that individual, the sociality corollary lays down one part of the individual's contract with others. Furthermore, that individual in the pursuit of making sense of his world is carrying out experiments, some of which are on other people, in order to validate his predictions. How can he validate or invalidate them if he does not have other people around on whom to carry out these experiments? He needs people, and may be therefore be said to be dependent upon them.

Problems arise, however, if our person puts all his eggs in one basket. In other words, if he depends on only one person for validation of all his social constructs, whatever their field of interest or activity. This is likely to become an intolerable burden for the person chosen, as well as being unlikely to provide effective validation for the individual in areas where perhaps his choice has little experience. A more healthy situation pertains when the person *disperses* his dependencies around a number of different people. A wife or partner for emotional and very personal issues; a work colleague for matters relating to work; the bank manager for financial issues; the wine merchant for choices of alcohol; and so forth. In such a situation, the person has a variety of appropriate people to depend upon for validation in discrete areas of expertise or interest. No-one feels put upon, and appropriate help is usually readily available.

The extreme of dispersion, of course, also leads to difficulties. This occurs when a person seeks out anybody or everybody for the validation of his or her predictions. Here is the passer-by, stopped in the street, and asked for advice or help. The dispersion has become too vague, with no attempt to match subject with expertise or understanding of the person approached. This kind of situation is also ripe for the development of hostility, and can lead to major difficulties all round.

With this notion of dependency such a contrast as *independence* suggests total social withdrawal with no attempts at social or individual validation occurring at all. This might be the hermit complex, where all attempts at outcome of experiment are sought from within the individual only. This is clearly not a pleasant or satisfactory state of affairs for most human beings, and is therefore not their choice. Some dispersion of dependency, however, is effective. It does not remove the individual's own ability to choose for himself, but does provide a useful range of validational experiences on which to base experiments.

No-one would begin to suggest, least of all ourselves, that what we have described so briefly above covers every possible type of construct, or process going on in an individual person. Clearly there must be more, some not even yet thought about or verbalised. However, those we have described are those found to be most useful so far in understanding how PCP deals with certain issues, and how we work in relation to seeking validation, making choices, elaborating our systems, and in terms of some of the difficulties or problems which can occur therein. In the chapters which follow, many of these areas will be discussed again, often in the context of a clinical or practical example. By the end of the book, we hope you will feel familiar and comfortable with them all.

5

WHAT CAN GO WRONG?

WHEN THINGS NO LONGER MAKE SENSE

It should be clear from earlier chapters that when we speak of things "not making sense" we are concerned with much more than any failure in our ability to *think* about things logically. There are many times in our lives when something happens to throw us seriously off course. We lose someone we love. We experience violent change through illness or accident. An important role in life is taken from us through retirement or redundancy, divorce or feeling no longer needed as a parent. We may fail badly in an area of importance to us. Less specifically perhaps and more gradually we realise that relationships have continually gone wrong; we can even see the pattern but not understand why we repeat it. In a threatening situation fears and anxieties we thought we had overcome re-emerge or, for no tangible reason, life seems to lose its meaning.

We may ask ourselves what's wrong with the world. We may ask what's wrong with us. The answer will to some extent depend on the kind of "theory of personality" we hold, such as those outlined in Chapter 3. If we are inclined to see ourselves as governed by Fate, we are more likely to look outside ourselves for the cause of our distress. If we believe that we have a part in creating who we are we will look inside. This may be a temporary state of affairs. Time, adjustment, the support of family and friends may gradually lead us to come to terms with what has happened and we are able to move on—changed, undoubtedly, but with a renewed energy and purpose.

For some of us, sometimes, however, the situation does not seem to change. The anxiety does not diminish and the distress, far from easing, is increased. We wonder whether we are ill or whether we are worthless, have done something wrong to bring this unhappiness on ourselves. If we think we are ill we will seek medical help from those who can give us drugs to make us feel better, or those who "treat" sick minds and hearts. Our wickedness, perhaps, can be cured by confession or prayer or making up for our sins by doing some good.

While by no means dismissing the value of medicine or spiritual help, this approach invites us also to explore how it is we feel as we do in relation to our ways of construing. In Chapter 4 we looked at how the person, described in terms of the system of construing developed over time, approaches events, making experiments, considering their outcomes, adjusting outdated "theories" in a continuous process of personal evolution. It is when this movement stops, when we are "stuck" without the means to deal with changes in our circumstances or confused by loss of definition of ourselves or loss of contact with others that we may need to question the functioning of that system, perhaps in quite radical ways.

In this chapter we shall look at some of the ways in which people find themselves trapped in distress and suggest where it might be in the nature of their construing of things that the major problem and therefore some kind of resolution might lie.

THE EXPERIENCE OF GRIEF

Loss of Another

Grief may come with the experience of all kinds of loss, but the loss of someone important in our lives can be the most devastating. For a young child, still dependent on a particular adult as its main source of security in a still-confusing world, the shattering effect is obvious. People who were too young fully to understand what has happened have recalled their sense of being abandoned. Some have experienced their first awareness of being a separate person, with the awe and terror that such knowledge may bring. Others may not remember the event at all, but difficulty with subsequent relationships in terms of extreme dependency or inability to allow themselves to get close to people, may give some idea of how they dealt with the death at some level at the time. For an older child or adult the loss of someone close can also result in a sense of the person's own diminishment, leaving an emptiness and incompleteness which is hard to put into words.

A number of people, such as Bowlby (13), have described various "stages" of grief. There is the initial numbness when the person does not fully believe what has happened. Then the phase of "yearning and searching for the lost figure"; some in this situation continue to see and hear the dead person or expect to find them waiting when they come home. It helps to talk to them as they always did. They want to talk about them and remember. They may seek help to get in touch with them, if they believe in a life after death. All of this is expressing a natural unwillingness to let go of someone we love. This may be followed by a period of "disorganisation and despair". And only later comes the development of "a greater or lesser degree of reorganisation".

The failure to work through grief may be looked at in terms of failure to move through such processes as these towards that necessary reorganisation or reconstruction of life. And it is helpful to try to see what is stopping the person from moving. In Chapter 4 we described Kelly's views of those states of transition such as anxiety, threat and guilt. These are often particularly relevant in a situation of loss, where strong anxiety in the face of such change is inevitable, where threat to one's sense of self, as we have said, is very common and where guilt or "dislodgement" from the self we thought we knew is often intense. If a person's role in relation to the one who has died is a central one, especially if it is the dominant role they play in their lives, this kind of guilt can prove unbearable. A woman is suddenly no longer a wife, a man a husband. A girl has no function any more as a daughter, a lover as a friend and sexual partner. For Bella, the loss of her mother was so devastating that she remained, as she said herself, "numb to feeling". It shocked her that she could neither weep for her nor feel anything except a dull flatness. When we explored her relationship with her mother it seemed clear that their intense interdependency kept

Bella's role as a daughter the most powerful force in her life, overriding friendships and love relationships. Without it, it was as if she herself had died and rather than confront such overwhelming loss of self she had become immobilised.

Ann, an older woman, experienced a similar loss of a central part of herself when her husband died. She no longer had a purpose in life and was almost overwhelmed by the anxiety of having to make decisions for herself, make choices which concerned her own needs alone. Her "solution" was depression, a state in which her world became so constricted that choices about what to do and how to handle the outside world became irrelevant. She stayed in the house looking at old photographs and reading letters over and over again. It was as if she remained "yearning and searching", not allowing herself to experience the disorganisation and despair.

To reconstruct your life after the loss of a child must surely be the most difficult process of all. Because of a child's dependency, death by accident or illness will raise questions in most parents as to their own responsibility. Construing their child as part of them, in a very real sense, the feeling of loss of something very central within them may make their guilt even more intense than in any other relationship. The senselessness of the death of a young child in particular faces the family with an event beyond most people's understanding and confusion and bitterness may be overwhelming. The event may call into question a parent's whole view of life and to "move on" from disorganisation and despair will involve fundamental change.

Loss of Self

One of the most painful losses we experience may come through illness or disablement. Here change may be sudden and violent and the sense of loss of the person that used to be is overwhelming. Linda Viney (14) describes the effect of illness and hospitalisation on "Alice". She is desperately trying to make sense of her new situation but has no past experience to help her. She has always seen herself as "the healthy one", she has never really considered the possibility of her own death before, she has never, as an adult, been in a position of such dependence and has lost her role as the pivotal figure in her family. She has to reconstrue herself in so many aspects that it is no wonder that she and many others in her position are confused and frightened. Others report the shattering effect of discovering themselves to have a chronic condition. If it is one which demands a complete change in life-style it will inevitably require new ways of looking at the self and the world. Many, of course, manage even radical change of this kind but some may continue to mourn for the rest of their lives.

The concept of "mental illness" is even harder for most people to deal with than that of "physical" illness. The prejudice born of fear that exists within many of us towards someone who has suffered, say, a psychotic breakdown of some kind is often echoed in the minds of those who have had the experience. The fear of "madness" is as old as time and memories of feeling out of control or driven by strange forces are not easy to come to terms with. Is there a weakness inside which caused it in the first place? Will it happen again? Family and friends may be watching for signs of recurrence. In many cases long-term medication is prescribed and the person's attitude to such dependency is important here. One man who had been deeply, suicidally depressed understood that the cause was basically chemical and that medication made up for a deficiency. He was able to take drugs in his stride and see himself as in control of his life, able to respond to early signs of difficulty by self-management. He likened it to being diabetic and in need of insulin. This is also possible for people with schizophrenia. If, however, medication is seen as something which controls the person utterly, then he or she will either fight against it or feel diminished through their need of it. We will look at the processes involved in some of these conditions in a later section.

In some instances, illness may more clearly cause the type of damage which directly affects the person's capacity to construe. Where brain-damage causes loss of perception, loss of language, loss of memory, for example, the person not only has a new situation to make sense of but is less equipped to reorganise his or her construing. Some of the bizarre behaviours seen in such people are often dismissed as simply signs of deterioration. We may look at them more usefully, however, as desperate attempts to find meaning amidst chaos. With this approach we are more likely to be able to tune in and relate to them in their search for themselves.

David Green (15) describes poignantly the strategies used to cope with this by some head-injured boys with whom he worked. Initially there was denial of what had happened to them, with angry assertion that they were as before. Then came an attempt "to wring some sort of advantage out of their plight" and, finally, most difficult of all, some were able to derive pride and self-respect from the achievements of the new self. Reconstruction of the self here demands tremendous courage and it is not surprising that some in this situation "will elect to live for ever in the world of fantasy and regret"—regret for what they were and what they might have become.

In members of the family of someone who is changed through illness or disablement there may be a similar course of grief to be run. A wife, too, for example, may deny the extent of the change in her husband and frantically seek one "cure" after another for his disability. The threat of her own change of role may be enormous, with not only full responsibility for children but the realisation of his dependency on her alone. The more mutually supportive the relationship has been before, the greater will be her anxiety at having to carry things on her own. A child who "loses" a parent in this way may experience great anger and despair at having been let down and this in turn increases the parent's guilt. The reconstruction of a family system after such an event can be a long and painful task.

We hope to have made it clear so far that these experiences of denial and despair, the strategies of constriction or frenzied activity, are not in themselves evidence of something "wrong" with a person's construing in the face of loss. They may in fact be seen as aspects of the reconstruction process itself. Only when someone becomes fixed in one way of dealing with the event and unable to move on can we perhaps say that their "system" of construing is failing them. In Figure 5.1 we outline the various processes which might be involved in the experience of grief.

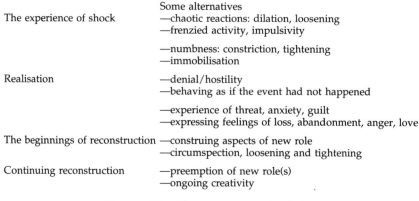

The experience of shock	Some alternatives —chaotic reactions: dilation, loosening —frenzied activity, impulsivity
	—numbness: constriction, tightening —immobilisation
Realisation	—denial/hostility —behaving as if the event had not happened
	—experience of threat, anxiety, guilt —expressing feelings of loss, abandonment, anger, love
The beginnings of reconstruction	—construing aspects of new role —circumspection, loosening and tightening
Continuing reconstruction	—preemption of new role(s) —ongoing creativity

Figure 5.1   The processes of grief

WHEN RELATIONSHIPS GO WRONG

Parents and Children

In Chapter 3 we spoke of some of the effects of early relationships on the development of children. Here we shall attempt to describe further what can go wrong in our construing of others and ourselves in relation to them. We touched on the importance of the mother's ability to make sense of her child and his or her needs and how the nature of those early interactions can influence the child's anticipations of others. We have shown how a child's self-construing may be affected by labelling, comparison with a sibling and the expectations others have or do not have of them. All this may provide a foundation for later experiences which it is hard to alter. Although we do not suggest that everything which subsequently goes wrong must be due to parental handling, there is no doubt that what a child makes of the relationship with either parent can form a pattern for sexual relationships, relationships with colleagues and, indeed, with their own children.

At thirty-six years old, Kate had had a number of long-term relationships with men, all of which had ended in her being rejected for someone else. She longed to be married and have children and the likelihood had begun to seem very small. She was depressed and could find little interest in other aspects of her life. When she talked of these relationships a pattern revealed itself of her becoming totally preoccupied by whomever she lived with at the time. She seemed always to be waiting—waiting for them to come home, waiting to know what they wanted next, waiting for the final blow to fall. She had seldom become angry when it happened. She assumed that she was just not a very interesting or lovable person and any man was bound to choose another sooner or later. Only when we related this poor valuation of herself to her experiences of rejection by her parents did the "inevitability" of her expectations make sense. Her father had never got over his disappointment that she was not a boy. Her mother lamented the fact that she was not a pretty girl. Either way, she could not win. To challenge and change this pattern she needed to reconstrue some aspects of herself and her own needs quite radically and learn to make her own demands on a relationship.

In contrast, Roger, while also experiencing one loss of relationship after another, chose to blame the women involved. They did not understand his needs. They were selfish and unpredictable, did not know how to sustain love. When he described various episodes in his life with them, there was the recurring theme of his being shocked by a sudden loss of temper on their part, or the discovery that they could have moods and periods of dissatisfaction of their own. It seemed that he had not only set each of them up to be the sort of person he needed but been completely unaware of the effect of his own behaviour on them. This inability to see things through another's eyes and persistence in assuming that all thought and felt as he did was the major cause of trouble. As a child he had suffered no obvious neglect or cruelty. But his parents did not communicate with one another or with him. Little feeling was expressed either of anger or joy and physical contact between the three of them was minimal. With no brothers or sisters and few friends Roger lacked early experience of coming to understand how others felt and had been given neither validation nor invalidation for his views of himself. Thus his extreme "self-centredness" was understandable.

It is possible to view Kate and Roger as being in complete contrast in their ways of construing themselves and others. Kate seemed only to exist in order to anticipate another's needs. Her view of herself depended on how far she succeeded in doing this. She had no boundaries. Roger, on the other hand, had little skill in sociality and lived very much behind a wall of self-absorption. Kate allowed herself to be invaded by others, Roger sought to impose his constructions of things on everyone he came in contact with. It is likely that their partners had found both approaches impossible to relate to and until a great deal of work had been done by each of them they shared the same fate of rejection and isolation.

It is only now, when the extent of physical and sexual abuse of children is beginning to come to light that the greatest damage to the growing child and the effects on future relationships is being more fully recognised. Not only do these children carry guilt into their adult lives but they may have great difficulty in construing alternative ways of relating to those outside the family. Against all evidence of caring and affection from others a girl may choose someone who behaves towards her as her father did, as if she can expect nothing else. A man may be attracted to a woman of violence like his own mother or bully his wife as his father bullied his. Some young men and women protect themselves from repetition of early pain by keeping their distance from all intimate contact. The secrecy so often involved in these experiences may make it even more difficult for them to talk about it later. Many believe that abuse cannot be erased and the task of rebuilding a self that can leave such suffering behind is a formidable one.

When you think back to your relationships with your own parents and other members of your family do you see any pattern repeated in later ones? They may not be bad, of course! Your expectations may be of support and understanding. If not, can you question whether you might be repeating these patterns unnecessarily? and can you, perhaps, put yourself in your parents' shoes in these early years and think what they might have meant by what they did or did not do? It might be possible to talk to them about it.

Couples

Although difficulties between sexual partners can often be traced back to early relationships, work with couples also shows that basic differences in ways of construing may be a cause. Joan and Robert had been married for seventeen years. Since they shared a value for "family", things went well while the children grew up and most of their attention was focused on them. When their three girls no longer needed them, however, and communication between them was more concerned with themselves, differences emerged which led to many misunderstandings. Joan was full of ideas and energy and filled her day with ceaseless activity. She rushed from one interest to another, wanting one moment to extend her artistic skills, the next to embark on a rigorous course of study. Without the focus of the girls' routine needs she constantly changed her mind about everything from meals, to projects for the house, to holidays. She found Robert's more structured approach to life infuriating. He liked consistency and to be able to predict what was happening. His views on life were much "tighter" and he found her constant changes a source of anxiety. Unless they could recognise and respect each other's very different ways of approaching things they were in danger of losing much that was precious to them both.

As we saw in the case of Roger, where one partner demands that the other fall in with his or her view of things there is bound to be trouble. Where *each* is involved in such demands, the result is disaster. They may never see and accept each other as they really are. Michael and Rosemary met soon after the break-up of their first marriages. They were both unhappy and bitter and found comfort in sharing their pain. Michael saw Rosemary as the caring, unselfish woman he had failed to find in his first wife. To Rosemary, Michael was the strong reliable man she had wanted all along. For a while things went well. Then he realised that other things were important to her besides him— her work, her own family, her friends. She was disappointed by his "weakness" in not tackling the neighbours about the noise they made and being too conciliatory when things went wrong with the repairs to the house. When, in an attempt to rescue things, they embarked on some PCP work, which involved writing their views of themselves, their views of each other and how each would like the other to be, it was clear that neither knew how the other felt and each wanted something the other could not give. Things which were important to Rosemary in a relationship were not even mentioned by Michael and their priorities in life were poles apart.

How do think your ways of construing things compares with that of a partner, past or present? Does one of you need things to be very predictable, one of you like to look at things from many angles? Do you cope with anxieties differently, one constricting to make things more manageable, the other becoming more chaotic when things go wrong? When you make decisions, does either of you tend to leap to a conclusion immediately or go round and round all the possible options? None of this need be a problem—if you can allow each other to be different.

Friendships

Much of what we bring to our sexual relationships we have learned through friendship as well as our relationships with our families. Working with children who are at school, we have found that, although they may present with problems to do with learning, with teachers or with difficulties at home, their preoccupation is often with peer relationships. It matters whether they are liked by others, it hurts when they are isolated, bullied or teased. One seven-year-old was referred because of temper-tantrums which his family found intolerable. His talk was of the friend who had let him down or the one who had stood up for him. He needed to begin to recognise the "rights" of others as well as himself and to be able to share attention. A child with a speech problem had gradually withdrawn from his class-mates because of teasing by one boy. When he learned to deal with him more effectively he began to feel part of the group again and establish a range of friendships.

So what is friendship and how is it similar to and different from a family relationship? We asked a group of 13/14-year-olds this question and they had no difficulty in saying what was important to them.

"You like the same things"
"You play together"
"They stick up for each other"
"They share what they've got"
"You know what they're thinking"
"They don't let you down"
"You can talk to a friend if you're miserable"
"They're fun to be with"
"You're not on your own"
"Friends help you out"
"Friends don't tell on you"

... and so on. The major theme in these responses seemed to be loyalty and as a group when we discussed it further, they were quite clear that it wasn't the same as with family. Yes, you might stick up for family but more because you "ought to". And you might not like any of the things your family did or even like them!

When these "rules" of friendship are broken a young person is deeply offended (so are we all later on). Most of the problems of young peer relationships are to do with being let down and for one friend to split on another is a mortal sin. The experience of this kind of unconditional acceptance of these rules is an important one and if a child misses out on it through isolation or for any other reason, he or she has missed out on a dimension of relating which may not be found in the family. It may indeed in some ways compensate for poor family relations and provide a basis for closeness and understanding which would otherwise have been lacking.

Young children cannot always put into words what is wrong for them. But they sometimes tell us through play or drawing. Michael, a shy nine-year-old who had begun to do badly at school and occasionally went home in the middle of the day could not say why. But when asked to draw a picture of when he was happy and when he was unhappy he produced the drawings shown in Figures 5.2 and 5.3 which he was then able to talk about.

Figure 5.2   "Happy" drawing

Figure 5.3   "Unhappy" drawing

The "happy" drawing (Figure 5.2) shows him playing in the park with a friend. There is no-one else around and there is a sense of space and freedom. The "unhappy" picture (Figure 5.3) shows a group of boys playing football with one standing apart, hiding behind a bush. When he talked about the second picture he said that he didn't like football, although he is playing with a ball in the first one. He didn't like so many people around and, above all, he didn't like changing with all the others.

Apparently football had started that term and it was the first time he had ever had to change in front of other boys. He had an older sister at home and mother had been very concerned that he should respect her privacy. Her approach seemed to have imbued some shame in him about his own body which mother had not realised. They were a gentle family and he had always found the roughness of other boys frightening and confusing. His friend in the first picture was "not noisy like the others" and didn't laugh at him. But he would have made little sense of the claims for friendship made by the group described above.

It is often useful with an adult client to look at their patterns of friendship as children. Although we all have a "best friend", some children seem to cling to just one other child from very early on. If something goes wrong, the child is shattered and takes a long time to build up a new relationship. These children often repeat this pattern as they grow older. They "put all their eggs in one basket" and form over-dependent relationships, unable to turn elsewhere for fulfilment of their needs. We often see that adults who find it hard to get close to others experienced this difficulty as children. In fact, they seem not to have learned the basic give and take which comes from quarrelling and making up; loving one minute and hating the next; feeling sad for someone or being pleased by something good that happens to them.

We spoke in Chapter 3 of the need for children to relate to a wide range of people outside the family in order to enhance their potential for self-development and have a more comprehensive set of views to test out as possibly valid for themselves. The experience of friendship remains important as we grow older. A couple who become completely absorbed in their children or their work may miss out on some aspects of continued growth. They may find it more and more difficult to comprehend the views of those outside the family and even respond with hostility to the "threat" of invasion by neighbours or others they have to come into contact with. The family construct system may be a narrow one as the children are likely also to turn to their parents or siblings only for validation. Such families find themselves isolated when things go wrong, not knowing who to turn to or how. They may find it especially difficult to comprehend ways other than their own and have no interest in people from different backgrounds or cultures. In the world of work they may make few and only superficial contacts.

> What sort of friendships did you have as a child and what part do you think the experience of these relationships played in your capacity for relating now and your sense of yourself?

Work Relationships

When someone complains of trouble with work, very often it is relationships with colleagues which are the problem rather than the work itself. Sometimes, of course, there may be a particular personality clash or lack of understanding between two people which has not been experienced before. In other cases, however, there seems to be a thread which runs through the whole of a person's working life. "The boss" is always found difficult and threatening. Peers are continually uncooperative or envious. Those working for them are bloody-minded or idle. If there are such themes it is important for the person to look at the patterns to try to clarify what is going on. What are their expectations in these relationships and are they appropriate? Are there aspects of their own behaviour which trigger off antagonism or cause confusion in the working environment?

Reams have been written about what makes a good and what makes a bad boss and, undoubtedly, most people will respond well to someone who knows what he or she is doing, can put themselves in their employees' shoes and know when to take charge and when to let people get on with things and so on. But a person who always has trouble with those in authority may not even respond to such qualities favourably. The chances are that they have their own axes to grind from way back and project their own threats and resentments on to anyone in that role from the beginning. Everyone from a critical father, teachers who expected something from you, and managers is construed in the same ways. Comments on work are taken as carping, praise is mistrusted. We have found that when clients are asked to describe what such people might be like they have great difficulty. They are only seeing in their behaviour what they have expected to see.

Working in partnership with others can be stimulating and enriching. Ideas are sparked off between you and abilities complement each other. For some, however, working with others is a strain. There may be a sense of being in constant competition, of being done down, of feeling inadequate. One young woman who had been deeply jealous of her attractive and easy-going brother, though very critical of herself and her irritability, always found fault with the way she was treated by colleagues. They did not value her enough. They would not listen to her complaints and obviously found her tense and prickly. She had to admit that it was the same everywhere.

Some people enjoy the responsibility of having others work for them. They go out of their way to get the most out of them and take pains to try to understand their point of view. Others can only lead by their own book, however, and find it irrelevant to seek such understanding. Construing what "should" be done tightly, any questioning is a threat. On the other hand, where a person is unsure and indecisive as to what is to be accomplished they may be equally uneasy in the face of suggestion. Neither of them is likely to establish that blend of professional and personal relationship which makes for fruitful cooperation. In all these relationships, the key factor seems to be sociality— the ability to construe the constructions of others at least in relation to the project in hand. It does not have to involve liking or having very much in common outside work itself. What is essential, however, is a basis of shared understanding of each others' roles, of the purpose of what is to be done and the means by which things may be accomplished.

> If you have problems relating to people at work, try to see whether it is simply the luck of the draw or whether there seems to be a recurring theme of difficulty.

LIVING WITH STRESS

The experience of grief and troubled relationships are probably the major causes of stress in our lives. But there are other factors which can bear down on us so hard that we feel ourselves failing to cope. Once again, our system of construing is in some way inadequate to deal with what we have to face and we may need both to modify our ways of approaching some things and invent quite new ways of meeting others. Children have to do this all the time as they grow up and experience an ever wider and more complex world. It is not always recognised that this process cannot end if we are to continue to develop and extend ourselves.

Troubles in School

A young child going to school for the first time has more than new relationships to deal with. There is a new environment, new things to learn. They may not be used to the noise of many voices or the size of the school building. They may find the routine of a stricter timetable, where they have to change what they are doing at the sound of a bell, frustrating. They may not understand at all why they are being taken from one room to another or sent out into the playground from time to time. Learning new skills can be exciting for some, but for others, more anxious, it can be a confusing nightmare. Children may be very stressed by their inability to do things and a particular activity may fill them with such dread that they would do anything rather than go to school. Many adults can remember something of those early days and all new beginnings may be for them just like those first days at school and bring them some of the old feelings of helplessness and confusion.

As with most situations in life, the majority of children manage their period of time at school, learning as they go, expanding their construing of things and creating themselves with a greater or lesser degree of success. For a minority, however, it may be a time of extreme stress. Apart from the difficulties in relating to their peers touched on earlier, some never come to terms with their teachers, find learning either irksome or traumatic and leave school with bitter memories and some damage to their growing sense of their own value.

Tom Ravenette (16) looks at trouble between teachers and pupils from a Kellyan point of view when he describes how referrals for help come out of the *teachers'* failure to make sense of the child's behaviour. Although children may well be disruptive, failing to learn, truanting or generally making nuisances of themselves, he is concerned with the teachers' experience of invalidation in those instances when they feel unable to do anything to change the situation. If a teacher has always construed himself or herself as "able to get on with children" or, worse still "liked by children", to find themselves on the opposite poles with respect to a particular child will be threatening and may well lead to an attitude of hostility towards that child.

In his work with schools, Ravenette not only explores the situation with the children themselves to find the source of their discontent and what means there are to change things, but also takes steps to encourage the teachers to look at the child's behaviour in a new light which does not challenge their own core constructs. A child may choose to "fight with teachers" because the unattractive alternative he sees is to "be a crawler". She may opt for "being late" or "playing hookey" because otherwise she would have to be "cooped up all day". Disrupting lessons by "playing the clown" may seen infinitely preferable to "being a swot". In order to change things, the child needs to find an acceptable alternative to the two options and the teacher needs to understand something of the child's own dilemma.

Learning difficulties in school may be a source of anguish to a child. The causes can, of course, be many. There may be a degree of handicap, extreme anxiety in the face of something new, a sense of inadequacy in comparison with a sibling or quicker friends. Many children may do reasonably well in classwork but panic when it comes to exams. Whatever the situation, trouble can accumulate until the child not only gets further and further behind but their construing of themselves as stupid or dull becomes confirmed in their own minds at least. This will have important implications for after school and unless something happens to change things their choices for work may be limited and the attitude of anticipated failure perpetuated. Occasionally a child will meet with a teacher who discovers some talent in them and helps them to approach things more effectively. A change of school may lead to a change in the child's view both of learning and of himself or herself. A new aim for the future and a sense of purpose can also spur an apparently dull child to achieve what no-one thought possible. Again, the crucial factor in terms of the alleviation of learning difficulty seems to lie in the understanding of how any child construes the situation and what, for him or her, is the real problem about it all.

Stress at Work

Ken Powell (17) has written a clear and comprehensive book on stress from a PCP point of view, with its major focus on the work situation. He points out:

> "You spend about forty hours of each week at work. Something like two hundred days a year are allocated to your working life. This major influence on how you live can create tensions of many different kinds. The way you perceive your responsibilities; work relationships; plus the actual tasks—their quantity, quality demanded and complexity may be major contributors to stress in your life."

He sets guidelines for us to explore our own personal stress factors in relation to certain themes which he has found commonly governing a person's approach to work:

(1) *Career*—work as career where success is important.

(2) *Instrumental*—a way of earning money to buy things which make life satisfying.

(3) *Security*—to provide basic security in life.

(4) *Vocation*—expressing your talents and aptitudes.

(5) *Doing your own thing*—a way of self-development and liberation.

(6) *Balance*—one part of life to be balanced with other aspects.

(7) *Taking what comes*—just accepting what's available, either as a positive choice or you feel that this is how it has to be.

(8) *Political*—seeing work as a political issue.

It will be clear that where one or any combination of these superordinate constructs are central to your perception of the meaning of "work" they will bring their own potentials for stress. If "success" is of primary importance then its contrast, "failure", may be particularly threatening for you. If work is seen as a "vocation" and it does not provide expression for your talents and aptitudes, there will be frustration and so on. There may be tensions between the demands of home and work, and there may be conflict between the demands made by work and other things which are important to you. And there are many issues around the nature of the work itself and a person's perception of his or her performance that can cause stress which we might define in personal construct terms as the awareness of conflict, leading to anxiety or even threat.

Ken Powell's book *Stress in Your Life* is particularly useful for those who find that things continually go wrong for them at work. In it he presents various ways of discovering your own stress factors and suggests means for dealing with them more effectively.

The Impact of Redundancy and Retirement

The threat of redundancy hangs over many people today. The very term with its implications of being no longer useful, superfluous, has a depressing ring and may be in itself a major cause of stress which affects not only the person involved but his or her family and close associates. When the feared event occurs, there must be a process of experience somewhat similar to grief—the shock, the confusion and panic, the attempt to reorganise or, sadly, if there appears to be no solution, a kind of resignation which may bring with it constriction and hopelessness. Much will depend on the way people generally see themselves and what happens to them as to how resilient they will be in the face of loss of role in work. If there is validation from other sources and a core sense of your own value, the energy it takes to set about reconstruing your position with regard to earning a living, using your abilities and maintaining self-respect will be there.

Where, however, there is no support but anger and anxiety from those dependent on you, the experience of guilt may be intolerable. Where self-esteem is fragile, old doubts about yourself may be confirmed. If a person's work role has been central to their way of life, loss of it will leave a void that nothing, for the time being at least, can fill. The structure of the days and weeks, the focus of much of our attention and interest, the companionship of colleagues are no longer there. It is no wonder that some people who are made redundant feel that life is not worth living. And yet others *are* able to pick themselves up, discover something new and elaborate themselves in fresh directions.

Retirement can be anticipated with feelings of impending liberation or the kind of threat which faces those who fear redundancy. Again, a person's sense of who he or she is and what he or she might become will govern these anticipations. And the experience, when it comes, will prove a shock or fulfil expectations, depending on how effective a person's predictive system is. Those who are able to see themselves ahead and picture what life will be like without work are probably in a better position to make the transition with relative ease. If they have looked at the implications of having more time on their hands, of being about the house more, of having less money, and how all this might affect others, they may have been able to plan a rich future for themselves. It is often the failure to predict the implications of change which leads to disappointment and discontent. Pre-retirement courses and counselling are often focused mainly on this issue of prediction and the reconstruction that will be needed to enjoy the altered circumstances.

Construing "Mental Illness"

So far we have looked at events in life which may be so challenging to the system of construing we have developed so far that, temporarily at least, we may be unable to deal with them effectively. This is what we have meant by the phrase "things go wrong". The constructions and processes which serve us reasonably well are inadequate to deal with what happens to us. Here we shall focus on situations in which it seems to be the system itself which is giving trouble. As Gavin Dunnett (18) has already pointed out, much has been written about the value or otherwise of the notion of "mental illness": whether it exists at all; whether it is an artefact of the society in which we live; what its boundaries are; and whether the medical model is right to treat it. Like a number of other construct theorists, while not suggesting we abandon the mental illness model, he urges us to explore alternatives. He himself, for example, has looked at phobias (19) in terms of how the "threator" (the spider, the lift, the high altitude) challenges and invalidates a whole network of our most central construing of ourselves.

Don Bannister (20) produced some of the earliest work in this area when he explored schizophrenic thought disorder in the light of the extremely loose construing to be found amongst those thus diagnosed. The implications here for treatment, that is, strengthening the person's ability to tighten, are very different from many current approaches. So too is his hypothesis as to the possible cause of the disorder of processing: "serial invalidation", by which is meant that the person has been subject to constant disconfirmation of their views of themselves and their worlds so that prediction becomes chaotic. The "symptoms" of delusions, hallucinations, mood swings and so on, may also be viewed from other angles. Suppose we apply the credulous approach to delusions, for example, and acknowledge that, to the person concerned, they *are* real? We may perhaps then be more in a position to put ourselves in their shoes and able to communicate with them on more common ground.

Dorothy Rowe (4) has also approached depression from the point of view of the processes involved in becoming depressed. While concerned with the content of a person's construing in terms of the metaphors used to express their situation, for example, she also draws our attention to the massive constriction which takes place, which she sees as a way of dealing with the anxiety, the chaos, which might otherwise have to be faced. If we withdraw from life, however bleak that option may seem, we cannot be expected to engage in the complexities of relating to others, striving for achievement or acknowledging the ills which lie outside ourselves. Eric Button (21), in a book significantly entitled *Personal Construct Theory and Mental Health,* with its emphasis on the contrast pole to mental illness, draws together a comprehensive body of work on what have usually been regarded as psychiatric disorders. The authors focus on features of the construing process which may be found in people suffering from these difficulties. A tightness of construing tends to be prevalent in all but schizophrenia and vulnerability to invalidation and the development of ineffective strategies to avoid it are common to them all, together with failure to anticipate others. In most, the problem area is more highly elaborated than any other aspect of the self. Peggy Dalton (22) has found in her work with stuttering that dilating the clients' focus beyond disfluency and helping them to construe themselves and others in much wider terms than speech performance has led to a reduction of preoccupation with speech alone and thus to a reduction in stuttering and an increase in general well-being.

We are not, then, suggesting that other approaches to "mental illness" should be discarded. There is no doubt that in some conditions such as depression and hypomania, medication plays an important part. What we are saying is that whatever else may be brought in to help in the management of these disorders, attention to and work with the person on the way they construe themselves and their problems is not only possible but needful. A great deal more needs to be done in this area by those working with personal construct theory but there seems no doubt that it has a new and significant dimension to offer.

Coming back to where this chapter began: we spoke of things going wrong in terms of events and ourselves no longer making sense. We emphasise that by this we mean at every level and not just in the head. Something happens to us which we haven't foreseen or which we have waited for with dread and, for a time at least, we do not know how to deal with the emptiness or the feelings aroused in us. Sometimes it may seem that only time or a change in circumstances can help us. But our contention is that, since we *do* have some choice about what we make of what happens to us, it is always possible to do something to change the state and the position we are in. We may never retrieve what we have lost of ourselves or another person. We can, however, go on to develop something new. This process need never end.

6

WHY SHOULD THIS APPROACH HELP ME?

We don't know who you are, of course, or how you come to be reading this book. We hoped, when we set out to write, that some of you might be therapists, social workers, teachers or psychologists but, as we stated, one very important aim is to make George Kelly's ideas more accessible to a wide range of people who may not have any specialised knowledge. We believe in our clients knowing what we are doing so one group of people particularly addressed are those who may feel that therapy would be useful to them. Others may simply have an interest in how we function as human beings and find this way of looking at personality meaningful. Whoever you are, we shall attempt in this chapter to show how this approach can help us all make more sense of things, whether we are deeply troubled or wanting to extend ourselves in more effective ways.

We hope it is clear from our earlier chapters that the various processes described as we attempt to understand what is happening to us are not in themselves seen as "pathological" or judged by any good/bad criteria. "Tight" construing is essential in some circumstances and limiting in others. Mostly, as we have said, we move continually through successive creativity cycles from tight to loose and back again. Extreme "constriction" has been shown as a feature of depression but this process, again, can be helpful where, for example, we are faced with too much material and need for the time being to focus more narrowly on things more nearly within our grasp. Although anxiety can be painful it may also provide a spur to make us review our situation and set about changing things. Temporary "hostility", or denial of what at some level we know to be true, may give us breathing space where we are not yet ready to reconstrue and is only damaging when a person clings to that position against all odds.

In our last chapter we were largely discussing how things might go wrong for all of us in the natural course of events and the effects these events might have on the ways in which we see ourselves and the world. In some instances we demonstrated how such events can affect us in the long term, while in others, we showed how a person might regain equilibrium and move on. Even where illness or serious loss has taken from us important aspects of our lives, it is still possible for us to develop and grow. The focus of the second of Kelly's volumes is on psychotherapy and we shall begin by discussing why we feel that his views on how people might be helped to overcome their difficulties has so much to offer someone in distress.

FOR CLIENTS AND PROFESSIONALS

If you are already trained in one of the helping professions you may feel that taking on a new philosophy and an alternative approach to therapy, counselling, or your role in a school or other institution could be confusing or too threatening to the ideas that have guided your work for some time. And, certainly, this may be a challenge—and it *has* been one which many have survived! At first it may seem as if you have to call in question everything you have been doing up until now and you have some kind of either/or choice between your original orientation and this one. But this is by no means the case. Many therapists trained in other schools have found that, although they do have to question *some* of their old ideas, personal construct psychology in fact helps to make more sense of much of what they do. Choice of technique may be made more clearly in the light of the diagnostic constructs Kelly provides. Issues such as "resistance" and "transference", which arise whatever approach is taken, may be better understood if viewed in relation to his constructs of transition (discussed in Chapter 4) or what he has to say about dependency.

In the end, most therapists who have undertaken training at the Centre for Personal Construct Psychology, for example, have found that their skills and theoretical understanding are enhanced through using PCT as a kind of "umbrella" which can make use of a wide range of procedures, whether they originate from psychoanalysis, Gestalt therapy or most other orientations. In turn, these therapists have contributed many ideas in the way of techniques to others in their training groups.

Within the therapeutic field itself PCT has attracted workers from many different disciplines. Gavin Dunnett's book *Working with People* (23) has chapters showing the development of the ideas within speech therapy, occupational therapy and social work, as well as clinical and educational psychology and counselling. One chapter also shows how PCP has influenced work in primary health care.

Hilda Browning, a social worker, expresses clearly why she herself chose PCP. She was told of Kelly's theory by a psychologist when she was airing her difficulties in accepting other psychological bases:

> "... while working with a multitude of people who differed radically from each other, each having his own context and unique situation—some of which might be within my own range of experience, although much was quite outside my own environment or manner of daily living. Each person, it seemed, demonstrated different capabilities and required an understanding a relationship which bore little resemblance to the ways in which I had engaged with the previous person ... None could be fitted, in a procrustean way, to a particular framework; rather, as I listened, did I detect something of the framework by which he ordered his life, whether or not to his or other's satisfaction."

Kelly's approach, not surprisingly, attracted her and she found that looking for the person's themes, entering the client's own world, seeing the client as the expert on himself, made sense of much that had been troubling her.

Recently, a physiotherapist working on a PCP course complained that it was all very well, but with the degree of handicap amongst the people she worked with and the relatively little time she spent with them, all these techniques for exploring the client's world were not relevant. She certainly could not use grids or self-characterisations (see Chapter 7) and most of her clients would not be able to put their "constructs" into words. As she continued the course, she realised that the approach did indeed have much in it for herself and her clients. Apart from the changes which occurred in her own perceptions of their situations, she recognised that words were *not* the be-all and end-all for understanding how other people experienced things. She became one of the most inventive members of the group in terms of finding means for facilitating and observing the ways in which people construed. Some of the non-verbal aspects of children's construing have been touched on and others will be described later.

As we shall see below, the probation and other services are also finding the approach helpful and we see no reason why the elaboration of Kelly's ideas should not continue.

If I Need Therapy: Why This?

There are a wide range of approaches to counselling and psychotherapy available for those who feel they need this kind of help. Some choose a particular approach because a friend has been helped by it, others are recommended by a doctor, perhaps, who favours one school of thought. Yet others, frankly, have no idea what is involved or assume that all approaches are similar. It seems a pity that so little information is available before someone meets a therapist as to how he or she views the process of assisting change in others. It is of little use to many to say that you are "analytical" or "client-centred" or "gestalt" after your name. Only other therapists are likely to know something of what the terms imply. As it is, unless it is part of a therapist's strategy during the first meeting (as it is with us) to convey as clearly as possible what the approach is, it may be some time before the client knows what is being aimed at.

Sometimes, of course, a prospective client has read a good deal and may well have a feeling for a particular therapy. Most of them have something to offer and there is no doubt that rational-emotive therapy, say, may suit one personality especially well and Jungian analysis another. It is our contention here, however, that personal construct therapy is so comprehensive in its range that it can help all those in need who really want to change—even those who don't, by clarifying the reasons why change may be unacceptable. This may seem a somewhat grandiose claim but our outline of the theory in Chapter 2 and all we have said subsequently should have conveyed the essential difference between this approach and some of the others which look at human distress in relatively narrow terms. Some, for example, consider all clients in relation to sexual difficulty, whatever their presenting complaint about themselves or their lives. Others look only to the earliest relationships for the source of the problem and, although we have seen how crucial these can be, such a view may be limiting. To focus only on making changes in behaviour may equally miss out on very important aspects of a person's way of living.

Personal Meaning and Change

Personal construct psychology does not bring any ready-made model of the meaning of "symptoms" to work with clients. With the essential focus on the person's *own* meanings, therapist and client explore the ways in which these views themselves might be keeping the person unable to change things for the better. Where, for example, someone believes that an unhappy experience in childhood is the cause of some current anxiety, it is important to look for the highly individual implications of that experience for clarification, rather than interpret in any generalised way. Janet was afraid of water—would not go in the sea or in a swimming pool. She had remembered an incident in a pool as a child when she had fallen in the deep end and nearly drowned. She had tried desensitisation, with no effect, and been told by one counsellor that she had an excessive need for control. It didn't really add up. When we looked at the incident more closely she began to connect the feeling of being abandoned with the extreme fear and recalled that her father was standing at the edge of the pool, not looking at her or hearing her cries. Earlier conversations had revealed a very important construct for Janet: *"protects me"* vs *"abandons me"* and there seemed to be some difficulty with dependency in all her relationships. Control or lack of it had not emerged as significant to her. This, then was the area we needed to work on.

Toni began to have panic attacks which made her unable to work in her job as a model. Out of the blue one day she had been waiting to go on at a very important fashion show, started to shake uncontrollably and was unable to walk. After this, almost any public place became difficult for her to cope with—restaurants, large shops, theatres. She had the sense that everyone was looking at her and she just wanted to run away. As a child, Toni had been extremely shy. She spoke of hiding behind furniture if people came to the house. Later, however, she learned to dance and with the help of a sympathetic teacher enjoyed performances and described herself as becoming "very confident" (the opposite pole to "shy"). Modelling held no fears for her and she saw herself as outgoing and happy. At the time of the first panic attack she had just broken off a relationship with the man she was going to marry and was very depressed. She didn't "feel herself" at all and it seemed that she had suddenly moved back to that other pole where all she wanted to do was hide. The aim here was to build some alternative to the *"shy* vs *confident"* choice which governed much of her picture of herself and made her vulnerable when things went wrong.

Construing Processes

These are just two small examples of how this approach attaches supreme importance to a person's construing of themselves without resorting to preconceived interpretations. Further examples will be given in later chapters. But content is only one aspect of the meaning things have for us and personal construct therapy pays as much attention to individual **ways** of construing as the material of which that construing is made.

The greatest problem may lie not so much in the views someone has of events but the way they approach them. A person may feel quite happy with the sort of work they do and have considerable skill but if, say, they have trouble making decisions (the CPC cycle) they may not express their talents effectively. Harry was a skilled engineering designer who nevertheless lost more than one job through his failure to complete work on time. He became stuck at the beginning of a task in an endless circle of circumspection, with so many possibilities open to him, unable to move on. He needed to learn the process of selection (pre-emption) in order to take the first step in what he was doing.

If someone's approach to life is governed by a notion of *"justice vs injustice"* they will find it hard to accept injustice both in themselves and others. Yet all of us are bound to be unjust from time to time and we may deal with this by the process of fragmentation described in Chapter 2. It is as if the left hand does not know what the right hand is doing. But there may come a time when one's own injustice cannot be denied. Chris had this strong belief in his own fairness and integrity but he was clashing badly with a colleague at work. He disliked what he described as his cavalier attitude, which went against his own meticulous attention to detail. Then a project in which they were both involved went badly wrong. Chris realised that he had made a serious miscalculation. But their manager jumped to the conclusion that the other man had been careless as usual and he was blamed. Chris was too afraid of the consequences of his actions to own up but awareness of the injustice of it all haunted him. His guilt was extreme and he called into question many of his former actions, especially in relation to work, where he felt he had fallen from his own high standards in this respect without acknowledging it to himself. He became very depressed and it took some time before he was able to restore himself and try to function less rigidly.

What Techniques do you Use?

This question is more often asked by other therapists than by clients, but we have occasionally been asked by prospective clients whether we "use dreams", "do hypnosis" or, once even, "do you do primal screaming?" Although the answer to that one was that we could not imagine a situation in which we would use primal screaming, to most other enquiries it would be "yes if it is relevant". The "techniques" of personal construct therapy are few. Procedures such as the self-characterisation or repertory grids (see Chapter 7) can be regarded as techniques, but otherwise the therapist will use whatever method seems appropriate to the person's need at the time. Thus, if it is felt that someone needs to loosen their construing, chain association, relaxation, dream material, drawing, role-playing, movement, any of these and many other methods may be included in sessions. Where, on the other hand, a person has difficulty tightening, he or she may be asked to clarify their construing by being more explicit, by summarising what they have been saying or doing, by putting a rather vague experience into historical context and so on. Role-play may be a tightening as well as a loosening process, depending on the form it takes.

It should be emphasised that the use of a wide range of techniques found in other approaches is by no means a random business. They are chosen in the light of what a person needs to do to facilitate change. Kelly (2) points out that:

> "The relationships between therapist and client and the techniques they employ may be as varied as the whole human repertory of relationships and techniques. It is the orchestration of techniques and the utilization of relationships in the ongoing process of living and profiting from experience that makes psychotherapy a contribution to human life."

The other important point to be made is that no technique should be applied if the client feels uncomfortable with it. Some people are embarrassed by role-play or have hang-ups about drawing. Whatever the therapist's fondness for either procedure, the clients' well-being comes first.

The Therapeutic Partnership

In Chapters 7 and 8 we shall be discussing the Kellyan approach to the relationship between therapist and client in some detail.

Here, though, we shall just describe it briefly as it seems an important factor in a person's choice of someone to work with on their difficulties. Don Bannister once gave a talk on therapy in which he outlined the various roles a therapist might play in relation to clients. There was the Priest-like figure, who laid down laws of living, the Just-a-Good-Friend, the Prestige figure, and so on. Kelly would have none of these but sees therapist and client as partners in the enterprise, each having their own area of expertise—the client being the expert on himself or herself, the therapist, hopefully, being the expert on helping them to explore their problems and set up experiments for change. No respectable counsellor gives "advice" and this is not the brief of a Kellyan therapist. He or she, while responsible for what goes on in sessions, leaves the responsibility for the clients' lives to them.

Inquiry and Experiment

Some therapies are more action-orientated than others. And personal construct therapy is by no means the only one to involve both parties strongly in the process. But as you will see in Chapters 7 and 8, personal construct therapy demands a great deal from both therapist and client. The stereotype of the client bringing his or her latest "thoughts" to the session, laying them at the therapist's feet to await "interpretation" is a far cry from the work that is done here. The initial exploration of the problem presented depends as much on the clients' willingness to elaborate their complaint and express how things seem to them as it does on the therapist's guidance as to what areas it might be important to focus on and how this can be done. Setting up experiments for change, too, is a joint activity and although it is the therapist's responsibility to see that the ventures are manageable, it is the client who carries them out and together they consider the outcomes.

A number of clients have expressed their relief to us when they found that we were *not* in the business of having all the answers and governing their lives for them. This notion had kept them away from therapy up until then. Others it is true, feeling desperate at the beginning of therapy were rather hoping that some superior wisdom was to be had which would solve everything for them without too much hassle on their part. But, in the end, most people rediscover their self-respect through what *they* are asked to contribute and from the feeling that *they* are solving their own problems and have learned something which will help them to manage things better in the future. When things are working well, we find that our clients are ahead of us in ideas for tackling areas of difficulty and, because it is *their* construing which is the focus of our concern, their capacity for invention and extension within their own lives becomes rightly greater than ours.

Responsibility

Ultimately, everyone has to acknowledge responsibility for their own views and actions. Early on in therapy, perhaps, a client may look to the therapist to clarify what this involves. But as time goes on it is important that such clarification is taken over. This may be particularly difficult for clients who have seen their difficulties as caused by others, by circumstances or even by sheer bad luck. Their most painful experience in therapy may be to take on board not only a sense of being largely in control of their current and future lives but how they might have made more effective choices in the past. But this approach, while encouraging people to reconstrue past actions, does not ask them to spend the rest of their lives feeling guilty about them or trying to "atone" for them. In fact, Kelly (1) makes a distinction between atonement and "repentance" in the true sense of the word:

> "not in the popular sense of self-abasement, but in its etymological sense of reconsideration or reconstruction."

It can happen that damaged relationships are mended when one person, as a result of therapy, begins to view another in a different light. That other may have been regarded as being to blame for all that has gone wrong and reflection allows the client to assume responsibility for a share of it. It may be, for example, that imagining a childhood situation from the mother's point of view at that time when she was young throws a different and more sympathetic light on how the mother behaved. A man of forty was still unable to forgive his parents for sending him away from home during the war. But when he saw a film of the devastation caused by the blitz in London, he was able to see what he had construed as rejection in terms of their wishing to protect him. Some clients come to realise that a parent or sibling who withdrew from them when they were young was going through some kind of trauma which they had not understood and had had to distance themselves from life as a whole.

Living our Lives

Perhaps the most important thing about the personal construct approach to therapy, however, is its concern not only for the presenting problem but for the enhancement of the person's life as a whole. As difficulties are explored so resources are highlighted. As problems are placed in the context of the functioning of the personality as a whole, clients often cease to view themselves solely in terms of that problem and begin to elaborate a picture of someone who can do and be things they had never even considered. This can be seen particularly in work with those who stutter. Often, they are so preoccupied with their disabling disfluency that everything else is of no account. Others also are construed largely in terms of their facility with speech. As their constructions of themselves and their fellows widens, other attributes, skills and qualities are attended to and a far more rounded concept of personality emerges. This process in itself plays a large part in decreasing the stuttering as it is no longer the central issue it once was.

Someone who has adopted an experimental attitude in relation to one aspect of themselves can become more adventurous in other areas. Learning to look at one thing from a variety of angles can lead to a more flexible approach to many things. Setting out to put yourself in the shoes of those who threaten you in order to understand more about them can develop your skill in sociality in general and make for better relationships all round. If, like Harry, mentioned earlier, work is done on decision-making because of difficulties at work, making choices in other areas of life will also benefit. Once a tight construer has learned to loosen or a loose construer to tighten up their constructions, the creative art is never lost.

So, as we shall see in the following sections, although the personal construct approach has therapy as its focus, its usefulness in every aspect of life is clear.

> If you are thinking of having therapy, don't be afraid to ask anyone you contact about their approach, their aims and the methods they use. Therapy should not be shrouded in mystery and, as the "consumer" you have a right to question and, if necessary, shop around.

PCP AND WORK WITH CHILDREN

It has often been pointed out that children themselves seldom present with problems. Usually, they are proving a problem to someone else—their parents or their teachers. A good deal of work has been done in recent years using the personal construct approach with parents and children as well as in schools to help teachers in their difficulties with pupils. We touched on some instances briefly in our last chapter. Here we shall look at some of the complaints about children and show how the processes of reconstruction applied in therapy with adults can help to clarify and improve the situation in the family and at school.

Trouble at Home

We have suggested earlier that trouble can come when children fail to fulfil the expectations of parents or there is a lack of understanding between them. Mothers are troubled by a child's disobedience, tantrums or behaviour such as bed-wetting. They cannot make sense of their passion for certain objects or their fear of certain people or events. They worry about their failure at school or their difficulty in making friends with other children. They are saddened by an apparent lack of interest or affection. If their child is handicapped, the parents may be unable to come to terms with their own feelings about it or to construe the child for what he or she is.

Most of the work undertaken with parents discussed in the literature is concerned with helping them to see things the way their children see them and thus understand why they do what they do and find ways of negotiating some change which is acceptable to all. Peggy Dalton (22), for example, describes the work with two mothers whose children had severe temper-tantrums. Here change was brought about through exploring the context of the outbursts, clarifying the part played by the parents and the rest of the family in the scenes and gradually reducing them by responding differently right at the beginning thus breaking the pattern in which all were locked. More significantly, in both instances there was evidence that false assumptions were made about the meaning of things to the child and understanding the implications of certain words, actions and attitudes for them played a crucial part in changing behaviour.

In the same paper, a series of sessions is described between the therapist, the mother and the child where the main objective was to help the mother to understand differences between her own construing and that of her seven-year-old son. These ranged from verbal meanings to concepts about relationships and the importance of doing things in a certain way. She had also feared that his opinion of her was as negative as her own, so finding herself wrong was a positive experience. At the same time, the child was encouraged to express and work through a number of fears through story-telling, drawing and imagining various different ways of dealing with them. The child did not see himself as having "problems"—only as being at odds with the family. The mother needed to look at her own difficulties instead of focusing on his.

Mancuso and Handin (24) have gone so far as to develop a training programme for parents to help them learn to construe their children's construing. With young children this may be enough to diminish many of the problems caused between them. With older children, however, it is important that they begin to see their parent's point of view over some issues. In the kind of family therapy described by Procter (25) all the members, parents and children alike, are involved in the attempt to understand each others' positions and meanings. It is this process, rather than any directive intervention on the part of the therapist which seems to have the beneficial effect.

Trouble at School

Tom Ravenette (16), as an educational psychologist, has been called upon to try to resolve things in the school rather than the family situation. He sees referral of a child by a teacher as related to the constructions which the teacher is putting on the child and its behaviour, and also the teacher's own important constructions about himself or herself, as we mentioned in Chapter 5. He believes that typically a referral can be reduced to one of four possibilities:

(1) "However I try to puzzle this child out I can never tell what he will do. He defeats my expectations."

With this referral the child's behaviour leads the teacher to question her understanding of children and at the same time suggests that her construction system is expected to deal with events which lie outside its range of convenience.

(2) "Whatever I do I am unable to influence what this child does either in how he behaves or in what he learns, even though my expectations are reasonable."

This child, therefore, represents a challenge to the teacher's sense of professional competence. There is also the suggestion that since the role relationship is not proceeding smoothly, there is a failure in the teacher's construction of the child's construing.

(3) "I was trained to teach normal children. This one is educationally subnormal or maladjusted...."

This referral suggests that the teacher has a rigid construction of himself as a teacher and an impermeable construction system for children in general.

> (4) "This child has problems but whilst he is with me things are all right. I am worried, however, as to what will happen in the future, either with a new teacher or a new school."

This teacher is implicitly saying that the child's behaviour lies within the range of convenience of her construction system, but that other teachers may well not see the child in the same way.

Ravenette suggests that a personal construct theory practitioner will have the following questions in mind when faced with a referral:

> (1) "What are the events which are the cause of the referral? Who is complained about? Who complains?"

> (2) "What are the constructions within which the complaint takes on meaning for the referrer, and what are the constructions of the child about his circumstances whereby he is complained about?"

> (3) "What are the ways in which the protagonist's constructions may be changed? Is there new information for old constructions or new constructions for old events? Is change to be encompassed through reflection or imagination, through experimental enquiry or directed role change? Is the main work to be done with the child, the referrer or both?"

Tom Ravenette exemplifies these basic questions in his approach to work with children and teachers in many papers written over the last decade and more. Don Bannister and colleagues Joyce Agnew and Sharon Jackson (26,27) have looked both at the development of children's construing of self and how this may be at variance with the views of those who teach them. Again, they found that children considered "problematic" by their teachers were not necessarily so viewed either by themselves or their peers and their own concern was far more in relation to other children than to their teachers. Popular children, it emerged, are clear about how they are seen by their peers, they are predictable in their responses, they agree with the view of others and use their constructs in the same way as other children. Whether they have trouble with their teachers is quite a separate and, to them, less important issue.

Young People on Probation

Increasingly, a personal construct approach is being used in helping young offenders. Those involved in the Probation Service and in Social Work are finding that by attempting to bring about change from *within* the construing systems of young people, instead of from without in relation to some specified set of rules of behaviour, more promising results are beginning to emerge. Pat Maitland's account of a conference on PCP, Deviancy and Social Work (28) held in 1988 shows the enormous range of application in this area. Work with those involved in shop-lifting, with drug abuse and sexual abuse, with those in residential care because "unmanageable" in the community, all showed much commonality in the stress laid on the youngsters' constructions of self and their difficulties in construing others. It does seem that development in these aspects of the construing process is more relevant than the external approach of social skills training, so popular in recent years.

The Young Mentally Handicapped

An alternative approach to both the education and the well-being of those with mental handicaps is long overdue. The work here is in its infancy, but, again, there is a new emphasis on exploring how these young people view things and what is important to *them*. Davis and Cunningham (29) give some telling examples of changes brought about through both professionals and parents attempting to see a young person's behaviour in the light of its meaning for *him*, rather than their own "socially acceptable" norms. In one instance, a child's attempts to touch boiling saucepans, construed originally as "getting at me for not taking notice of her", became reconstrued as attempts to help, because similar actions and facial expressions were observed when mother was cleaning or ironing. Setting up a pretend stove in the kitchen solved the problem. In another, parents who had previously construed hand-flapping as just a piece of stereotyped behaviour, reconstrued it as communicating excitement and were able to use the same action to communicate their own feelings to the child.

A particularly important finding here from research into the nature of the construing of mentally handicapped people was that their systems are undifferentiated and relatively simple in structure. Since this is likely to result in a failure to discriminate important aspects of situations, the suggestion is that it is important to simplify the environment, marking the significance of those aspects which are important and thus helping them to discriminate more effectively, rather than providing more and more stimulation, which is so often taken to be the need. These authors believe that PCT is especially useful in this area because it has application not only to people designated mentally handicapped but to the people, parents or professionals working with them. Needless to say, all that we have said with regard to mentally handicapped children also applies to adults.

PCT IN MANAGEMENT AND INDUSTRY

We referred briefly in Chapter 5 to things which can go wrong in the work situation. In some instances, it is clear that the availability of counselling, particularly in the larger organisations, could prevent some of the personal distress caused by the work itself, misunderstandings between people, impending changes in structure and work patterns. George O'Connor (30), discusses both the benefits and the pitfalls of establishing such a service in organisations. He points out that the values and goals in counselling may not easily be reconciled with the economic, rationalistic models which underlie organisational procedures and processes. The personnel practitioner here may have to ask "does the organisation we represent have a causal part in the creation of the employees difficulties?" He suggests that one of the personnel practitioner's skills must be to anticipate problems which might result from organisational structures or change strategies. Thus he or she plays a preventative role. He sees such a person as needing both a basic understanding of psychology related to individuals and of organisational psychology. A clear distinction should also be made between the counselling aspect of the work and the necessary "advising, telling or manipulating" which is part of the personnel manager's job. He himself, and others working in industry, have found personal construct psychology to be particularly useful in this setting.

John Porter, too, (31) emphasises the importance of developing understanding between management and employees, looking at the issue of motivation. In his study, he took as his starting point the hypothesis that every individual is different and that organisations may also be viewed as "individuals", each with well-defined construct hierarchies. Groups of workers and customers can also be seen as having group construct systems. The hypothesis that each of the above components have "individual" or unique systems would seem to imply that conflict or lack of harmony and satisfaction is highly likely. Here we can see the focus shifting from the difficulties of one or two people involved in the work situation to the structure of the organisation as a whole and the effects of its functioning on all concerned. PCP is increasingly being used as an approach in exploring and resolving organisational as well as personal problems. And when we remember the enormous scope of Kelly's own application of his theory including his work for the Human Ecology Fund on a range of international problems referred to in Chapter 1 we can only feel that we are still a long way behind him in what is being done all these years later.

However, besides a whole section devoted to the development of the ideas in industrial settings, Fay Fransella and Laurie Thomas (32) do show something of the scope of the theory's application in their book based on the International Congress on PCP at Cambridge in 1985. Papers on education take us far beyond the problems between teachers and children and consider new ways of learning. Others consider "attitudes and beliefs" in the light of these ideas, and yet others reflect on various aspects of the arts from a PCP point of view.

HOW THIS APPROACH HAS HELPED US

It seems appropriate, since this is above all a reflexive theory, to end this chapter with an account of how PCP has helped us, the authors. Each of us came to it originally in relation to our professional work and we do find we have a good deal of commonality in our understanding of it. But we are two very distinct individuals and the paths we have travelled since we began to understand and use the approach have inevitably also been separate and individual.

Peggy Dalton

I have written in Gavin Dunnett's book, *Working with People* (23) of how dissatisfaction with aspects of my training as a speech therapist led me to look for some kind of psychological framework through which to make sense of what I was trying to do. It seemed to me that we were taught to "treat" the disorders with very little reference to understanding the people who had to cope with them. We were armed with "batteries" of tests and treatment programmes which took no account of the nature of the persons with whom we aimed to make sometimes quite profound changes. If the programme "didn't work" either the clients weren't putting their hearts into it or we needed to turn to another programme and try again. And at no stage were we helped to look at ourselves.

In my special area of interest, stuttering, it became clear that something much more was required if people were to make such a radical change as that from stuttering to fluency—something which looked more deeply at the implications of change for each person for a start and which acknowledged the importance of understanding the person as a whole before attempting to modify one aspect of his or her behaviour. When I read Fay Fransella's pivotal book on her research into stuttering from a personal construct perspective (33), I had the feeling I had found it. What I did not realise then was the profound effect Kelly's work was to have on me as time went on.

To begin with, as I studied theory and practice, it was very much in the interests of the clients I worked with. It soon became clear that this was not only an approach which was useful in relation to people who stuttered. It could enhance every aspect of work whether with children or adults and whatever the presenting speech, voice or language problem. It wasn't a matter of "applying" it, like some external balm, in cases where there appeared to be a particular need for counselling. It was about understanding people and planning strategies for change with them in the light of *who they were and how they saw things* at the time, regardless of whether they experienced psychological difficulties or not. It was equally relevant to teaching and relating to colleagues. It simply made enormous sense to work in this way.

It wasn't possible to leave it as something I only related to others for long, however. Although, in our training in PCP, unlike much other training, there is no stipulation that we should have therapy ourselves, reflexivity is so crucial a part of learning that, inevitably, exploration of the ways in which we function and experiments to change aspects of ourselves which we find ineffective become part of the whole process. The support given for this in the training courses and supervision can enable a student of PCP to transform his or her ways of going about things. Certainly it changed me as a therapist to begin with. Since then, it has helped me in my life as a whole.

A few years ago my husband suddenly became ill and suffered brain-damage as a result. This event altered our lives in ways which we could never have anticipated and called for massive reconstruction on both our parts. At first, it was the whole notion of attempting to put myself in my husband's shoes which was the greatest help to me. I was more able to cope with confused and strange behaviour through trying to understand the meaning of that behaviour for him. With a severe memory problem, he was locked into the present and experienced extreme anxiety and threat as a result. Retaining awareness of things in the present he also suffered devastating loss of role in every direction. It was possible to talk to him about some of the feelings involved and together make sense of his constructions of things, which were dismissed by some as simply bizarre or some kind of "confabulation". It was clear that he was actively elaborating himself in a new role and deeply involved in the process of reconstruction. My part in all this was not that of a therapist or counsellor. That isn't possible with someone close to you. But there is no doubt that viewing what was happening to us from a Kellyan viewpoint was far more helpful than the entirely external judgements we were given by neurologists and the psychologists responsible for assessment.

At the same time, of course, my own role had changed radically and much of what I did, thought and felt had to be reformed. I too experienced threat and anxiety, hostility and guilt. I too could never be the same but had to move on from regret for what had been lost to the construction of something new. That process continues and I feel sure that it would have been a great deal harder without the support not only of other people but of an approach to life which is essentially forward-looking and creative.

Gavin Dunnett

PCP seems to have been so much part of my life and for so long now, it is difficult to look back and see how such an interest developed. I had originally trained as a doctor in Aberdeen, and for a very short period flirted with the idea of surgery as a career before opting for what was always my first choice, psychiatry.

I was interested in psychiatry for a number of reasons. First it was a relatively young branch of medicine with few prescriptive treatments. It seemed that there would be more openings for someone who wanted to try new ideas and be innovative than in the more traditional specialities. Second, I was interested in people, not parts. My attraction to psychiatry was because I thought it could be holistic and see the person's psychological problems in the context of their whole life situation. Concurrently with entering my psychiatric career I was a local government councillor, and I was astonished by the similarity between those who approached me with problems as a councillor and those who approached me as a psychiatrist. The initial decision as to whether to take the political or psychiatric route seemed quite arbitrary, despite the similar problems. However, the outcome for the individuals was often vastly different.

Third was the fact that the anti-psychiatry movement was waxing eloquent. Authors such as Laing, Goffman and others were challenging the whole basis of modern psychiatry. Despite much resistance, this onslaught was provoking change and so the whole spectrum became full of possibilities and an encouragement to be radical. Being radical or even anarchic is not something encouraged in the medical profession generally.

I had previously read fairly widely in psychology, and read more Freud, Rogers, Bateson, Ellis and others as part of my studying for specialist exams. But despite flirtations with psychoanalytic theory on the one hand and bioenergetics on the other, I remember feeling very frustrated that there didn't seem to be a theory at hand which was comprehensive, consistent and personal. That wasn't to say nothing worked—it often did—but there was no overall framework within which to operate.

It was at this point that a psychologist colleague rather fortuitously proposed doing a repertory grid on one of my patients. I had no idea what this was, but as it was explained to me, I began to get excited by the existence of a theory which produced such a technique. Not many people seemed to know a lot about PCP where I was, but the more I discovered, the more I felt I had found a theory of personality which was about people.

Shortly after this, I moved from Aberdeen to Dumfries and there had the great good fortune to have the opportunity of working alongside Miller Mair. He encouraged and stimulated my interest in PCP in far too many ways for me to be able to acknowledge here. Suffice to say I had found my framework for a serious, effective, but radical approach to psychiatry. Not only did it make sense to me, it seemed to make more sense to my clients. And it allowed me to make sense of the context in which I and they operated.

I spent two years in Dumfries before moving to London. At this stage of my career I was looking both for a base to move on to become a consultant and also for the opportunity to broaden my experience in as many ways as I could find. Moving to London was a gigantic experiment on my part and one which took some time to be fully validated. Again I was lucky—soon after my arrival. Fay Fransella started a training group in PCP, the first two of which became the forerunners of the Centre for Personal Construct Psychology. Here was an opportunity in a group setting to explore the therapy aspects of the theory rigorously. Increasingly, too, it seemed to be useful to me in my life as a whole. I began to feel as though I could understand my construct system in a whole range of areas of my living and this understanding was proving very helpful. Amongst other things, it allowed me to remain in a profession where the opportunity to practise as I wished seemed increasingly restricted (a fact which has not been reduced over subsequent years).

Increasingly I began to write about and teach PCP, initially with much trepidation, but subsequently and principally with the support of the late and much-loved Don Bannister, with more confidence. By now the effects of PCP have permeated my entire life although not to the exclusion of other ideas. As the title of this book indicates, it seems to have provided me with a psychology for living *my* life.

In conclusion, I would like to mention two enormous compliments I have received in the past few years. At one of the feedback sessions after lecturing on PCP to the Sheffield Psychotherapy Diploma Course, one of the students said to me—"I don't know about PCP; I don't know if I understand it; I do know I would be happy to be in therapy with you and that says something about your approach". The second compliment was paid by a student who attended a Winter School on clinical uses of PCP which I ran with Peggy Dalton for the PCP Centre.

Near the end of the course, we were exploring constructs for one another, and this student described me as a "post-anarchist". Somehow this felt exactly right: that although I could contend with chaos, I had moved on beyond it but could still live with it. For better or worse, both compliments seem to me to reflect my debt to PCP and the influence it has had on me personally as well as professionally.

7

WHAT DO YOU
DO TO ME?

There are two important points to be made at the outset of
this chapter. The first is that this book is written for both
professionals and clients. This means that the perspective might
seem to be different at times. After all, a professional worker
in whatever discipline cannot be expected to see things the
same way as a client ... or can he? The answer to this rather
fundamental question is a qualified "yes". PCP is reflexive.
That is to say a person using it to explain or understand
someone else is himself operating by the same psychological
processes as the person on the receiving end. Of course the
content of each construction system may be quite different,
and the way in which the two people make use of it also
different, but the principles which they use to make sense of
what is going on around them are the same. So in the context
of therapy and counselling, which was the original focus for
Kelly's approach although it has spread considerably further
since then, the question of "What do you do to me?" applies to
both counsellor and client. Each of them will be "doing things"
to each other, and each of them will be using their own construct
systems to make sense of what is happening. It is important to
remember that any interaction between two people who are
making some attempts to understand each other's construction
system (sociality corollary) leads to each playing a social role
in relation to the other, and this in turn may lead to changes in
both construct systems.

One example of this is the different kind of reactions this
chapter's title may have on an "average" professional or an
"average" client. Most professional counsellors want to know

what they are going to do in the sessions with their clients. They want to know what techniques to use to assist the process of change; how best to begin to understand their client; and what to do if things begin to go wrong. The client by contrast wants to know whether they are going to get any help, and if so, by what means. Both client and therapist want to feel comfortable with each other, and to feel that they can work together. The client probably expects to "have something done to her" but not to do much "doing" themselves; conversely the professional may well not be expecting much to be "done to him" but will be expecting to do quite a lot to or with the client.

Each of these two views on the same situation are quite valid within the constructions made by the two people involved. It is, however, immediately apparent that one or both will have to change in some ways to enable progress to be made. In fact, the probability is that both will change, and the purpose of this chapter is to look at the ways this occurs when precipitated by the second party in the interaction—that is to say, by the person *you* are interacting with, whether you are professional or client.

The second point to remember is that both parties in this enterprise, whether it be therapy, or supervision, or in education or wherever, are experimenting with the situation in which they find themselves. This notion can be frightening for both professional and client, although in fact it ought to be reassuring.

You will remember that PCP is about individuals making sense of their worlds by creating hypotheses, testing them out, and then incorporating the results of these experiments into their own personal construct systems. Where the experiments have produced repeated validation of a particular construction, or group of constructions, then the degree of likelihood of serious invalidation in a new but similar situation to those previously experimented with is very small. This is the professional's position. Over previous months and years he has worked with a range of clients, and has developed how he goes about it quite successfully. (If it were totally unsuccessful, one would hope he would not still be working in this field!) But *you* are a new client to this professional, and so the process he undertakes with you is yet another in a long series of experiments to check out that the way he works does in fact assist people coming to ask for help. At the same time, this professional has to be aware that although the techniques available are fairly well validated, they now have to be used in a totally unique situation, that of this particular client, and this particular client's construction system.

For the client, this experiment is probably more scary. Unlike the professional who has been this way before with other clients, this situation may be totally new. Help is being asked for which is itself a new way of trying to deal with the difficulties being experienced, whatever they are. The very fact of asking for help from a source not previously tapped is an experiment. From the client's point of view this may be an exciting way forward, a terrifying prospect enforced by circumstance, or simply an anxiety-provoking unknown. Nonetheless it is a major experiment which is being undertaken and which may have profound effects on the client's construction system.

Thus for both client and professional the situation is one of experiment. It should be reassuring for the client to know that the professional has to re-evaluate his or her procedures with this particular client, and listen to the unique position this client is in. It is not going to be a sausage factory approach. For the professional, the client's experiment is reassuring because there is a indication of willingness to change, to try something different. Both need each other to progress their individual experiments; both will learn from each other in the process; and both, if everything goes well, should enjoy the interaction.

THE CLIENT'S PERSPECTIVE

Whether you are a client coming for therapy, a student asking for guidance or supervision, a child going to a teacher or any other similar situation, you will come with some preconceived ideas of what is going to happen to you. These are your anticipations and predictions and often one of the first things that happens is that some or all of them are invalidated.

Let us give an example. Margaret was a middle-aged lady who had had some psychiatric treatment when younger but has been fine for many years, coping with marriage, children and a part-time job. Recently, however, there have been financial pressures at home, leading to strains in the marriage, and the development of a range of anxiety symptoms. Reassurance from her GP has not helped, and he has now, with her agreement, referred her to a counsellor.

Margaret's previous contact with a psychiatric/psychological service was fairly traditional for the time. She was seen by a doctor, given some medication, and effectively told what to do in order to get better. And indeed, she did get better, so this type of approach seemed to be validated for her. Not very surprisingly, therefore, when she first came for counselling her anticipation was that she was going to be told what to do in order to "get better". She was anticipating a directive therapist/counsellor who would pinpoint the problems, analyse the symptoms and on the basis of years of experience, cure her. For Margaret, along with many other clients, the reality was somewhat different. And although in some ways this new reality seemed to have some attractions—such as feeling individually valued—it also seemed rather threatening as well. It just was not quite what she was expecting.

Many clients, of course, just don't know what to expect. Sometimes, depending on their route to the professional they are seeing, advice and information has been provided on the way. A GP may have discussed what counselling involves before making a referral; friends having undergone counselling may share their experiences; a colleague having had supervision from a senior member of staff may describe what happened. But all these are second-hand descriptions at best. They are all viewing what you, as client, are about to get involved in from the perspective of their construct systems and their problems. And that is different from yours. So, however well clients may feel themselves to be prepared, almost inevitably some anticipations and predictions are going to be invalidated. Thus one of the first actions likely to occur, after introductions, is for your anticipations to be explored. Just what do *you* expect from this encounter, and from those which will probably follow. Most people expect when asking for help from a professional to be listened to, at least initially when outlining the problems.

However, a PCP-trained professional is not just going to listen passively to you. He or she wants to begin immediately to understand *your* world from *your* perspective. This is why your anticipations of the process you are both undertaking is the first area of interest. If you don't agree on what is being undertaken, or it is wrongly assumed that you are in agreement, awful misunderstandings may occur which can totally undermine the process later on. The fact that one wants help and the other is in the business of providing help is not enough. Some mutual understanding of what is wanted on the one hand, and how it may be supplied on the other is important from the beginning.

This first interaction also makes clear that the focus of the process is *your* views on the world, and that this is what the professional concerned is going to be principally interested in.

Up to now, the discussion has centred round "a professional" and "a client", and we have made the point that the client may be a whole variety of different kinds of people approaching professionals of various disciplines for different kinds of help. Whatever kind of client you are, the processes described below are going to occur in some form or another at some time or another in your interaction. However, the original focus of PCP was counselling/therapy, and so for ease of writing and presentation we are going to assume for the rest of this chapter that we are talking about a client/therapist interaction. Another point to make now, which may have already become apparent from the introduction, and the discussion above about anticipations, is that the title of this chapter is rather misleading. Many clients do come with the view "What will you do to me?" or, slightly better, "What can you do for me?". In fact, what actually happens is the answer to the question "What can you do *with* me?". It is a joint venture and although both parties experience the other as doing various things, the process is of mutual interaction. Along with a discussion of your anticipations and predictions, this sharing is likely to be an early point for discussion.

It is clearly not going to be possible to outline all the possible interactions or eventualities that may occur between you and your counsellor. After all, the process as we have outlined it is one of experiment. The range of possibilities for the counsellor to suggest to you is, if not infinite, at least very extensive. But before any suggestions for change, or practical "doing" type experiments are undertaken, the therapist has to have a firm basis for understanding *your* view of the world, *your* constructs, and the system in which *you* organise them. This is the process of subsuming: in other words, your therapist will use a variety of techniques and discussion to tease out your constructs and the way you use them. It is only after he has achieved effective progress in this stage that he can begin to see what may be going wrong *in your system*. Thus your first experiences are going to be about your expectations and then about you and your view on the world.

Many people find that attempting to examine themselves is a rather frightening and anxiety-provoking task. But with PCP the process only proceeds at the pace set by yourself. No-one is going to be bombarding you with interpretations or explanations or judgements or directions. For most clients, these initial sessions of exploration, so important for the therapist's understanding of you, are themselves fascinating ways of discovering about yourself. It should be interesting, enjoyable, sometimes surprising, occasionally distressing. Remember that the process is one of partnership and exploration. You have not handed over control to the therapist to do what she wills with you. You can still say "Stop, this is too painful for the moment". This is not to say that the subject will not be raised again, in a later session, but you are still entitled to protect your vulnerabilities, at least until you feel safe enough to explore them too.

So far we have discussed what may happen to you in generalities. Before going on to some of the specific techniques you are likely to encounter, we would like to re-emphasise the overriding generality that the entire process of PCP is personal to *you*. Whatever techniques are used, discussions are initiated, experiments proposed, results evaluated, *you* and *your* construct system is the focus of the work. This is why it is PERSONAL Construct Psychology.

What follows now is by no means an exhaustive review

of techniques available for understanding your construct system. Gavin Dunnett's book *Working with People* (23) gives a more detailed insight into the way various different clinical disciplines have used the theory in practice. But the five areas below are to us the most likely ones you will encounter.

1. Eliciting Constructs

You remember that a construct is the basic unit of your construct system. It is a form of discrimination between elements, and therefore as an element cannot be one characteristic without not being another, a construct has two ends, or poles. These two poles are not necessarily opposites but are contrasts which you use and which make sense to you personally. Some of your constructs have verbal labels to enable you to talk about them, while others may not have verbal labels, either because they were formed before you had speech, or because you have never needed to attach a label to them. An example of the latter might be the situation in which you have a "gut feeling" about someone or something. You know what it is you feel, but you cannot express it in words. Or at least, you haven't up until now! Construct poles are given names to distinguish them—the emergent pole and the contrast pole, but more of that below.

Now that we have reminded you what a construct is, we will explore how are they found. For a start, our speech and conversation is littered with them. "It's a sunny day today" infers you have a construct about weather—sunny vs something. In this case, "sunny" is the emergent pole of the construct rather simply because it has emerged first. If your counsellor were concerned to know the contrast pole of the construct, you might be asked something like "What kind of day is one that is not sunny?" to which the answer might be "rainy". Thus from simply conversation, one construct has been elicited:

Sunny (emergent pole) vs Rainy (contrast pole)

Thus even as you converse with your counsellor, you may discover yourself being stopped and asked, curiously, "You mentioned that you thought Mrs Bloggs was a slob. Can you think of someone whom you wouldn't call a slob? And, if so, how would you describe them?" Here the emergent pole of your construct is "a slob" while the contrast pole might, for the sake of example, be "a perfectionist".

Slob (emergent pole) vs Perfectionist (contrast)

There are three quick points to be made here. First, you can begin to see even from these simple examples how your discriminations are beginning to be discovered, in the first example in relation to weather, and in the second in relation to some people. Your therapist is seeking to understand the ways you sort out people, things and events, in order to predict their behaviour or actions. The second point follows on from this. The first example applied to the weather, while the second applied to people. This is the range of convenience of your construct. Describing Mrs Bloggs as either rainy or sunny is unlikely to be much help to you, any more than trying to differentiate the weather between being a slob or a perfectionist. The third point is that the examples above have nice neat verbal labels—sunny, rainy, slob and perfectionist. But you may find you need a phrase, sentence or even paragraph to try to explain what you mean. For example, one client asked to describe how she felt, replied: "I have a kind of a feeling of everything going well and smoothly as though on rubber wheels". This was a very evocative description of the emergent pole of that particular construct. And whenever we wanted to explore that again, the same sentence was used to evoke the feeling. With constructs that you have not given verbal labels to before, and especially more abstract constructs, you may find yourself struggling to find words to express what you feel or perceive. You may look to your therapist to help out, and feel rather frustrated when he doesn't supply a word or a phrase for you. But that would only be his word or phrase, not yours, and he will more likely try to encourage you and prompt you to produce your own. And thereafter, it will be your own words he will come back to whenever referring to that particular construct.

This process of teasing out constructs is known as eliciting. What we have described above might be described as "informal" eliciting. It is taken out of ordinary conversation.

However, eliciting can be done more formally (in its most structured way, for a repertory grid—see below).

Imagine that you are being asked to explore the constructs you have about different types of people. Some of these may crop up in conversation as above, but your therapist may want to explore this area more systematically. Between you, you may agree a number of people whom you can visualise, either by name or by role title. Let us imagine you have agreed on six kinds of person—lawyer, truck driver, housewife, bank clerk, traffic warden and dancer. You agree that you have some notions about each of these. You may then be given three of them by your therapist, say the truck driver, traffic warden and dancer, and be asked to think of a way in which two of them are alike but different from the third. You probably have to shuffle them around a bit in your mind, and puzzle a little, but eventually you might come up with something like "the traffic warden and the truck driver are both *practical*". You will then be asked how that differs from the dancer. "The dancer is *artistic*". Hence a construct of:

Practical (emergent) vs Artistic (contrast)

Now you may be given a further three people, housewife, lawyer and traffic warden, for example, and the process repeated. This time, you might come up with the lawyer and traffic warden *working for a living*, while the housewife is *working for the family*. As you are given each different set of three people, so another construct is uncovered until a whole series of different discriminations have been built up. This method is known as the triadic (i.e. in threes) method of elicitation and is very effective. It can be used for any group of elements; people you know, work situations, past events, physical symptoms or whatever. Indeed, any group of things about which you and your therapist are interested to discover your construing.

2. *Laddering*

Constructs are the basic units of the framework of your personal construct system, and you have now seen how some of them may be elicited from you. But you will also remember that the construct system framework extends both "upwards" and "downwards"—that is to say towards more superordinate constructs on the one hand and towards more subordinate constructs on the other. Superordinate constructs tend to be more abstract while subordinate ones tend to be more concrete.

The constructs elicited from you may be anywhere in that hierarchy of your system and isolated constructs unrelated to the system as a whole do not tell very much about the system as a whole. There are therefore two techniques for exploring either the superordinate connections of a construct (laddering) or the subordinate connections (pyramiding—see below).

Let us take for our example the construct elicited before:

Slob vs Perfectionist

This discrimination tells us something about how you distinguish between people, but tells us nothing about why. What reasons do you have for making such a discrimination. Why is it important to you to distinguish between people in this kind of way? Of course, part of the answer is to do with anticipation and prediction, but the other part is because you have some overriding concerns which make this particular discrimination important. The process of laddering is to explore these overriding, superordinate, abstract constructs. These are also likely to be ones where there is no simple verbal label. You know what you mean, but may well have to struggle to put it into words.

A typical dialogue might go somewhat as follows:

THERAPIST: OK, so you have a construct of *slob* versus *perfectionist*. Which would you rather be yourself—a slob or a perfectionist?
CLIENT: Oh that's easy—I'd rather be a slob!
THERAPIST: Why is it important to you to be the kind of person who is a slob?
CLIENT: Because a slob is someone who isn't bound by rules all the time.
THERAPIST: Someone who isn't bound by rules all the time?
CLIENT: Yes, that's it.

THERAPIST: So what kind of person is someone who is bound by rules all the time?

CLIENT: Someone with a strong sense of moral rectitude.

THERAPIST: Which kind of person would you prefer to be—someone who isn't bound by rules all the time or someone with a strong sense of moral rectitude?

CLIENT: Someone who isn't bound by the rules all the time.

THERAPIST: And why is it important to you to be the kind of person who isn't bound by the rules all the time?

CLIENT: Because ... (long pause) ... because it allows me freedom to make choices.

THERAPIST: And what kind of person would be one who does not have freedom to make choices?

CLIENT: Umm ...

Now this dialogue illustrates a number of things. First, the therapist has encouraged the client to look at the superordinate construct to being a slob. Initially it may be surprising that the client chooses the slob alternative, but as the superordinates are explored it becomes more obvious. If you see things in terms of:

Not living by rules vs Moral rectitude

then being a slob might well be a preferable lifestyle. Notice that the therapist checks out the words the client uses to make sure that he's got them right, and that the client is happy with his answer. Then having achieved this first superordinate level, the therapist repeats the procedure. Now the client finds the going altogether tougher. It's much harder to come up with the reason why, for him, it is more important to be someone who doesn't live by the rules. Eventually the phrase "freedom to make choices" is offered, but when the therapist tries to find the contrast pole, the client is stuck.

You can see, however, that a lot of information has been obtained, for both therapist and client. *"Freedom to make choices"*—a pretty abstract notion—is revealed as an important construct for the client, even if the contrast pole cannot be verbalised. It also adds to the information on *"slob"* which many people might automatically assume to be negative, but in this context is seen by the client as positive and preferable. This is why the therapist will be continually checking out with you to make sure he or she understands your meaning.

3. Pyramiding

This is the opposite process to that of laddering. It is trying to discover the subordinate structure, the more concrete constructs of what something is, or how it can be recognised. If we remain with our example of *slob* vs *perfectionist*, the dialogue might go something like:

THERAPIST: Let's look at what you actually mean by a slob. What kind of person is a slob? How would you recognise one in the street, for example?

CLIENT: Well, they wouldn't care about their appearance for one thing.

THERAPIST: Do you mean physical appearance, or dress or what?

CLIENT: Oh no, I just meant their dress. Their hygiene would be OK.

THERAPIST: What would be the contrast to someone who didn't care about their appearance?

CLIENT: Someone always well dressed—natty even.

THERAPIST: OK. So what kind of person is one who doesn't care about his appearance?

CLIENT: Someone who dresses comfortably—old jeans, sweaters, trainers, that kind of thing.

THERAPIST: And the natty dresser?

CLIENT: Always in suits and ties and polished shoes.

In this interchange, cut down to conserve space, it is clear that the client is increasingly encouraged to define exactly *what* he means by his constructs. In contrast to laddering, where the questioning is about *why*, here the questions are more *what* and *how*.

The reason the technique is called pyramiding is the way it is usually written down.

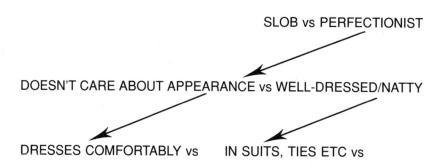

Each pole of the original construct can be treated the same way, and then those of the constructs derived from the pyramiding and so forth until a very concrete picture of exactly what a slob or a perfectionist actually is can be built up.

Using the process of elicitation to get at constructs applying to different groups of elements, and then laddering and pyramiding those constructs, quite a wide range of parts of the construct system can be accessed quickly.

4. The Self-characterisation

Along with eliciting individual constructs, laddering and pyramiding them, it is highly likely you will be asked to complete a self-characterisation. If you were called, say, Harry Brown, then it would probably be introduced to you as follows:

I want you to write a character sketch of Harry Brown, just as if he were the principal actor in a play. Write it as it might be written by a friend who knew him very *intimately* and very *sympathetically*, perhaps better than anyone ever really could know him. Be sure to write it in the third person. For example, start out by saying, "Harry Brown is ..." (1)

Many clients feel quite worried by being asked to do some writing, especially about themselves. Your therapist should try to reassure you by telling you that it doesn't have to be of any particular length, or contain any particular information. Also, that it is yours, and it is up to you whether, when you have finished it, you want to share it with your therapist. Obviously it may help him if you do, but you don't have to. Kelly wrote a whole chapter on the analysis of self-characterisation, some 40 pages, and this is not the place to go through that. If you try doing it yourself—say at the end of reading this section— you can begin to see some constructs, or at least their emergent poles, peering out at you. You can then explore those further by finding a contrast pole, laddering and/or pyramiding. In other words, it is an excellent method of accessing your constructs about yourself. You may also notice some themes, or particular issues which you raise. These give areas for the therapist to explore.

In our clinical practice, we have received many hundreds of self-characterisations, all of them different, all of them unique. In most cases, the client, themselves have been interested in what they have written—often they have had the sensation that their pen has run away with their thoughts. Not all self-characterisations received have been in prose writing. We have received poetry and painting, and one of us on another, and extremely daunting, occasion, music!

There is no judgement about what you write. Nobody is going to mark spelling mistakes with a red pencil or correct your grammar. It is straightforwardly and simply an excellent introduction to a particular set of constructs—those which you hold about yourself.

There are a number of variations of the self-characterisation. Miller Mair wrote a chapter entitled 'The community of self'(34) in which he explored the idea that each of us sees ourselves as a community of different "people" all interacting with each other. For example, one man might see himself as husband, car mechanic, bread-winner, father, gardener and so forth. A self-characterisation could be asked for each of the different selves seen.

5. Grids

To many people, PCP and grids are virtually synonymous. They have seen that the vast majority of published research using PCP relates to one form of grid or another, and assume that this is what it is all about! You should by now have realised that this is not so. A grid—or, to give it its original technical name by Kelly, the role construct repertory test—is at its simplest merely a tool for looking at how an individual uses a set of constructs in relation to one another.

Now this may sound complicated, and indeed it can be. There are many different kinds of grids derived from the original, and many different sets of complex computer programs written to carry out mathematical analyses of them. There are also several books written specifically on grids if you want to find out more: Slater (35), Fransella and Bannister (36), Stewart and Stewart (37), Beail (38). However, from the viewpoint of the client, the process is fairly straightforward as we have already covered some of the fundamental processes.

The purpose of the grid is to look at the way you use a set of constructs in relation to a given set of elements. Kelly's original was called the *role* construct repertory test because he was interested in the constructs used in relation to a collection of people defined by their role. In fact, he used 15 role titles, including (to take the first three as examples)

Your mother or the person who has played the part of a mother in your life.

Your father or the person who has played the part of a father in your life.

Your brother nearest you in age. If you have no brother, the person who is most like one.

and so forth.

Later on he includes people such as

A person with whom you have been closely associated, who for some unexplainable reason, appeared to dislike you.

and

The most intelligent person you know personally.

You would be asked to put names of people from your own life to each of these role titles, a different name for each so that there is no duplication. Once you have all fifteen, then the next stage is to use these as elements to elicit constructs about them. The purpose of starting with the role titles rather than simply asking you to think of 15 people you know is to ensure a wide range of different types of people in your sample, as well as make sure some of the most important and influential ones are represented.

The process of elicitation here is as described in the triadic method above. As we shall see this may be modified in special circumstances, such as with children. You will be given three of the names at a time, and asked in what important way are two of these three people alike, and, at the same time, essentially different from the third. When you have come up with something you will be asked to write it down, and then asked for the contrast to it. This is then repeated for further groups of three until between 10 and 20 constructs have been elicited. The next stage is to ask you to apply each of the constructs elicited to all of the people in your sample. And this is where the grid comes in. In order to indicate which pole of each construct applies to each person, a matrix of elements (always shown across the top) against constructs is drawn.

Thus if the elements are E1 to E15, then these are across the top while the constructs C1 to C15, each with an emergent and a contrast pole are put down the side, as shown in Figure 7.1.

Now there are a number of ways in which you may be asked to complete the grid. The most common nowadays is the rated grid. In this situation you will be asked to consider each element in turn, and to rate (usually on a scale of 1 to 7) where you think that person lies on each construct in turn.

For example, if the first element is "mother" and the first construct is "slob vs perfectionist", then you would be asked to ascribe 1 if you thought your mother was really a slob, 4 if you really did not think the construct applied to your mother at all, and 7 if you really thought she was a total perfectionist. Obviously you would use the other gradings if you didn't feel such extremes were appropriate. Having done that, you would then be asked to carry out the same process on element 2, then element 3 and so forth. When you had completed all 15 elements in relation to the first construct, the process is repeated with the

Scale 1 — 4 — 7	Mother (1)	Father (2)	Jo (3)	Mary (4)	Me now (5)	Tutor (6)	Geoff (7)	Alice (8)	As I'd like to be (9)	Grandmother (10)	Robert (11)	Joyce (12)	Trevor (13)	Aunt Joan (14)	Dr James (15)	
1 slob																perfectionist
2 successful																a failure
3 lonely																popular
4 not bound by rules																moral rectitude
5 friendly																unfriendly
6 can make choices																feel powerless
7 confident																lacks confidence
8 dull																lively
9 in control of life																out of control
10 intelligent																stupid
11 cares what others think																self-assured
12 generous																mean
13 unimaginative																has flair
14 easy to relate to																closed
15 bigheaded																knows true worth

Figure 7.1 Example of a grid matrix

second, then third and so forth, until the entire matrix of the grid is completed. (Some examples of completed grids are given in Chapter 10.)

This probably sounds extremely complicated and long-winded, and as though it would take a very long time to do, but in practice, it does not take as long as you would imagine, and once the idea of what you are doing is grasped, it is very easy to complete. So what happens next? In the case of a rated grid such as that described above, your therapist will probably take it away at the end of one session and return at the beginning of the next with a vast computer print-out! DON'T PANIC! It is amazing the effect that a computer print-out has on some people, most especially those who have had little or no contact with computers before. Essentially (and very simplistically) all that the various programs do with your grid is to work out the mathematical relationships between your constructs, and your elements. If you were to look at your completed grid yourself, you may notice some patterns emerging as to how you use your constructs. Perhaps all your male elements score at one pole of a construct while all the female elements at the other. You may then notice another construct which you seem to use in much the same way with only minor differences. Clearly in a 15 by 15 grid, it would be extremely difficult to see all the relationships visually, so we get a computer program to look at it mathematically and statistically.

Both the relationships amongst your constructs, and those amongst your elements can be highlighted, as in the example of Fran's main group of elements on page 192. Where you yourself are in relation to the other elements (people), and in relation to your ideal self, may be of interest. How you use particular constructs, which are the most important, and some measure of their superordinacy can be demonstrated. All this will, however, be discussed with you, and checked out that it makes sense to *you*. In many ways the purpose of doing a grid for the therapist is to confirm ideas he may already have, and to give an opportunity for both of you to check them out. Do not let yourself be frightened by the apparent complexity. Remember that a grid is only another tool to help you and your therapist explore your construct system more effectively.

Some General Comments

It is worth repeating again that the techniques mentioned above are only some of those which may be used in your sessions, and on the whole are designed to help you and your therapist decide and agree upon what your problem is, and to begin to plan how to tackle it. PCP does not have a strict recipe of actions to follow because it is personally directed. Thus your therapist is going to have to tailor his approach to you and what you can respond to and feel safe with. Any description of what may happen to you has to be seen within that context. Remember that *you* are a partner in the enterprise, along with your professional/therapist and that it is always *your* system that is the focus of attention.

THE PROFESSIONAL'S PERSPECTIVE

The majority of this chapter has already been composed of the client's perspective of what you, the professional, are going to "do" to him or her. And since the focus of the enterprise upon which you are both engaged relates principally to the client, this is right and proper. However, it is often wrongly assumed that this is the only way in which this interaction can or should be looked at. There is almost a conspiracy of silence about what client's do to their professionals/therapists. Either they are not meant to do anything at all, but remain passive tools of the therapists' abilities; or else the therapist is assumed by virtue of being professional to be impervious to anything that may occur. The former notion has already been debunked by our insistence that the process is one of equality and partnership. Certainly each of you bring different experiences and expertise to the partnership, but it remains a partnership nonetheless. The latter notion, that of the imperviousness of the therapist, is one that often seems allied to the construct of being a professional. Somehow whatever your client does, it will not affect *you*.

This is clearly rubbish. This interaction is an experiment for you too, although maybe with less at stake. How your client reacts, behaves, emotes, progresses will affect you, and the way you construe, and not just within the confines of your professional constructs. Fine, say some therapists, we have learnt a lot from our clients. Therapy is a rewarding experience. We enjoy it.

Here we have at least an acknowledgement that our clients do something to us, but amazingly it all seems to be a positive experience! Therapists and professionals in general are always filled with warm loving thoughts and everything in the garden is coming up blooming.

What is extremely hard for many professionals to grasp is the reflexivity of personal construct psychology. Yes, they have a professional set of constructs to operate as a rulebook in their encounters with their clients. Yes, they have core role constructs about themselves as professionals. But somehow they often seem to behave as though in the context of professional/client interaction, that is *all* they are. The idea that your processes are psychologically channelised in exactly the same way as anybody else's, and that this can go wrong or be affected just as anybody else's, is rather an alien one. So the first point for you-as-professional to take on board is that your client can do something to you.

The first area to discuss has already been referred to above. This is that the result of your experiment—that your approach will be helpful to your client—is validated. In other words, you manage to help your client, and you feel good about it. Most therapists do feel more than just that their therapy was good. They themselves feel good, validated as a professional, and validated as a person who owns that professional subsystem. There is nothing wrong in this. Indeed, without some validation, you would progressively begin to doubt your ability and efficacy until eventually you might choose to leave the profession or take up something different. Positive validation from your client is important to professionals who are after all human too.

What happens, however, when you get negative validation from your client, or, worse, when your client actively seems to do things to make matters worse. Most therapists have found themselves in this situation, and there are in some places methods for dealing with it outside the therapy situation. Supervision with a more experienced colleague, sensitivity groups and peer discussion may all contribute support for the professional. Support is needed for the professional to contend with what he or she construes as emanating from the client.

There are some clients who cannot be helped. Many therapists appear to find such a statement incompatible with their construction of being a professional. (Finn Tschudi's ABC technique explained in Chapter 9 may be of benefit here in discovering why!) So when faced with a client who does not change, or who appears to prefer the status quo to some apparently beneficial change, the therapist needs to look at his own construing of the situation as well as that of the client. Frustration, despair, anger are all emotions felt by therapists in relation to some of their clients. It may be that you are not an effective therapist. It may also be that you are not listening to what it is your client is telling you. Either way it is you, yourselves, that are going to have to deal with what is happening.

The second point to be aware of is that you may be faced with hostility. Remember that we discussed hostility back in Chapter 4 where we defined it in PCP terms as "the continued effort to extort validational evidence in favour of a type of social prediction which has already been recognised as a failure". Being on the receiving end of hostility from whatever source is an extremely unpleasant experience. Somehow you end up feeling that whatever you do it is never the right thing: it never seems to achieve the object you intended; it never has a positive outcome. Now this can occur in relation to the client's interaction with a therapist. It does not have to be deliberate, at least not consciously so, but if unrecognised, it can engender strong feelings in the therapist.

Let us give a couple of brief examples. At the beginning of this chapter we emphasised the need to check out the anticipations of client and therapist to ensure that both were viewing the interaction in a broadly compatible way. A client who attends but persistently seems not to hear the therapist's explanation of what is on offer and keeps repeating and demanding that their own anticipations are met is not a rare person. While the therapist will initially re-explain, and then try to understand why it is important for the client to cling onto these notions, continued hostility may lead to total frustration. The key here is to remember that the interaction is a partnership for the professional as well as the client, and the professional faced with an immovably hostile client has the right to withdraw from the partnership in the same way that the client faced with what he perceives as an immovably unhelpful therapist also has the right to withdraw.

The second example occurs when client and therapist cannot agree on what the problem is. Some clients with physical symptoms of anxiety or depression cannot accept that there is a psychological cause for them rather than a physical one. Sometimes they have "done the rounds" of a variety of physical doctors and have only ended up being referred for therapy as an apparent last resort. They continue to demand proper treatment of their physical symptoms, and while some may be prepared with the encouragement of the therapist to engage in the "What if it were psychological?" experiment, others may not. Faced with this kind of situation, the therapist has to decide eventually whether to continue to work with the client or not. Unfortunately, in some instances that choice does not seem to be allowed to the therapist, and it is in these situations that frustration can develop to a serious degree.

The object of outlining these examples, and indeed of adding this section to the chapter is not to suggest that clients are all ghastly or indeed wonderful, any more than therapists are all ghastly or wonderful either, but to remind you that you have feelings and constructs and a construct system too, and that you are allowed and entitled to recognise the effect that a client has upon it. You may have different responsibilities relating to how to respond to these situations, and these will be discussed in the next chapter. PCP is reflexive, and this demands an acknowledgment of personal humanity on both sides of the encounter.

8

WHAT DO I HAVE TO DO?

Whereas the last chapter was about looking at what was likely to, or could, happen to you, either as professional or client, in a professional/client interaction, this chapter is about what you yourself should be doing. In the same way as in the previous chapter, we propose to look at this from the perspective of client and therapist separately, although it must be remembered that some aspects may overlap and whichever role you see yourself as taking, the other is worth reading for you.

If there is one word that can be taken as a keynote for this chapter it is responsibility. The importance of this has already been stressed, but it will be elaborated here. One of the principal tenets of PCP is that responsibility remains personal. You, client or professional, remain responsible for the construction of your perception of reality and neither party in the transaction should be in the business of removing that responsibility. Each of you creates your own reality; each of you can change it if you want to. Equally you can choose not to change it. What you cannot do, in broad general terms, is blame somebody else for it, attempt to disown it, or make someone else be responsible for your actions. The price you pay for having choice is that it is you who are lumbered with it. Having choice implies that you have to decide which choice to make, and take the consequences of that choice into account in making future choices.

None of which is to say that you cannot seek help in making choices, especially those for which you have little data of your own to assist your decision. But asking for information, clarification, support or whatever still leaves the choice and its responsibility firmly with you.

Responsibility tends to be a rather hackneyed word in our modern society, as well as one often bandied around by politicians. As a result it has tended to absorb connotations which are not always those which are intended in this context. We thought therefore that it might be of interest to examine our constructs of responsibility to attempt to clarify for you what it meant to us. We were lucky in discovering we had a commonality of construing in this area!

Responsibility is the emergent pole of the construct. The contrast pole would be not owning your constructions. Laddering this construct led as follows:

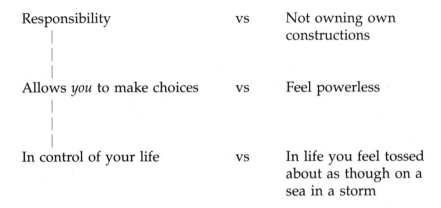

Responsibility	vs	Not owning own constructions
Allows *you* to make choices	vs	Feel powerless
In control of your life	vs	In life you feel tossed about as though on a sea in a storm

This ladder is, of course, based on the preferred pole being that you want to be the kind of person who takes responsibility, and thus makes personal choices, and ultimately is in control of your own life. For some people this extremely fundamental option is one which they are attempting to avoid, and one of the first tasks of any therapist faced with a client who is not owning their own constructions might be to explore their version of the above ladder. It may be that they are choosing the contrast poles because the assumption of personal responsibility carries with it too much anxiety or threat. Clients may not be aware of this avoidance, or may simply never have considered themselves as having a choice in this matter. Indeed this may be the very reason why therapy has been sought, although the presenting complaints/symptoms are likely to have been rather more practical and concrete.

The purpose of this explanation of "responsibility" at the outset of this chapter is to attempt to reassure you that, although you will be expected to own your own constructions, that does not imply a "you simply have to pull yourself together" type approach when in difficulties. No-one's personal construct system always works faultlessly, and sometimes they can get into a real muddle. PCP is non-judgemental. No-one will blame you (at least not within the client–professional axis) but you will be expected to accept that *your* life is in *your* hands.

And remember, these comments apply precisely as much to the professionals as to the clients. Neither side can cop out!

THE CLIENT'S PERSPECTIVE

What you have to do, as a client, involves (a) acceptance of responsibility, (b) being prepared to explore, (c) listening, (d) experimenting, and (e) learning. This sounds quite a formidable list, but if you think of the issues which have been raised about personal construct therapy over the past few chapters, then none of them should come as any surprise to you. The order in which they are presented is not particularly significant although it is likely that you will face them in the given order.

(a) Acceptance of Responsibility

We have already discussed this to some extent in the introduction to this chapter. There is, however, one important point remaining to be made. What you have to accept responsibility for is *your perception* of reality, not reality itself. It is what you make of your circumstances that we are concerned with. No-one suggests that you can alter the entire world to suit yourself. What you can do is to alter the way you look at it, and what it means for you, in order to enable you to make more productive and creative choices in the future.

This distinction between true reality and your perception and construction of that reality is very important. PCP is not a magic wand approach. It won't suddenly transport you to sunnier climes, find you an ideal partner, resolve your financial problems or bring back someone you are grieving for. But if for some reason you have become stuck in your life, unable to see any choices for yourself in a particular area (or even overall) then this approach can help you to find out why, free the blockage, and give you some opportunity for movement away from wherever you are.

This encouragement to change perceptions applies in whatever field you find yourself as client. The client with the therapist obviously needs to find out what he or she perceives at the outset in order to understand why it feels so terrible. The therapist who is a client in relation to a supervisor may need to understand his perceptions of his own clients and how they may be obstructing his ability to provide effective help. The client in business needs to review his own perceptions about how the business is running and the important issues involved before making any changes. In each and every situation, *you* as client have to start out by accepting responsibility for the constructions you have already made, and for what you have been doing with those constructions. This is the bedrock from which change is possible. Unwillingness to accept this, or refusal, makes further alterations almost impossible— which may of course be precisely the intention of the person refusing!

(b) Being Prepared to Explore

Once you have accepted that your constructions of events and circumstances around you are *yours*, you have to face up to the fact that you probably do not know, consciously, what many of them are. Up until now, you have possibly lived in a world where you felt things happened to you, or that you felt obliged to make certain decisions or take certain actions without clearly knowing why. Most of us do a fair bit of this all the time— it would become an impossible task to attempt to investigate all the constructs in play over every little action or decision in our lives. We would rapidly become totally bogged down (as indeed some people do who try). Accepting that they are our perceptions which colour our world demands that, where we do not like that colour, or where it seems to be causing us problems, we need to explore those constructs and perceptions in some detail.

This process of exploration, some of the techniques of which we discussed in the previous chapter, provokes various responses in clients. You may find yourself excited by the process, fascinated to discover the linkages and views you held without ever having really thought about them. You may become totally absorbed in the exploration, chasing new lines of interest incessantly, building up a bigger and broader picture of your construct system all the while. Remember, however, that there is a purpose behind this exploration in whatever role as client you have. Here exploration has a focus. It is not being undertaken purely for fun.

While some people, even in the midst of their problems, find this exploration fun, many others find it in varying degrees quite painful. You will remember that in an earlier chapter we discussed the PCP ideas of anxiety and threat. Both of these may be relevant here. It is not just being faced with external changes to one's construct system that can provoke anxiety. And detailed examination of your core role constructs—the very constructs that identify you as yourself—can be extremely threatening. All the more so if, as the process of exploration continues, it becomes obvious that changes need to be made. Threat can also occur where changes happen due to certain constructs, of which you were hitherto unaware, becoming available to you with increasing awareness. And further, not only may anxiety and threat be present during exploration, so also may guilt— the realisation that you have not always been acting according to the way you would expect yourself to act. Threat, anxiety and guilt are powerful emotions which have the tendency to reduce your desire to explore further. Yet it is probably at just those points where these feelings are most strong, that detailed exploration is most valuable or needed. What you have to do is to try and stick with it. You are, however, entitled to have some expectations fulfilled. First, you have a professional to help you with this process—you are not on your own. Second, you have the right to say "stop". Not, hopefully, "Stop I want to get off," but "Stop, I need a breather before I can go any further". Time out to consolidate what you have discovered about yourself before exploring further is entirely reasonable. Being prepared to explore does not imply rushing headlong down the exploration trail regardless of consequences. Both you and the professional you are working with have a set of brakes. Feel free to use them.

(c) Listening

Up to now, what you have been expected to do has been fairly active. You have to positively accept your role in creating your perception of reality, and you have to positively embark on exploring what precisely that perception is. Indeed, one of the fundamental tenets of PCP is that it involves you as client being actively involved in the processes. Listening, however, carries with it a more passive connotation. Or does it? In this context, listening involves both what you are saying and what the professional is saying to you. It is extremely easy, especially when under pressure, or in distress, to simply pour out grief, or frustration, or anger, or whatever emotion appears most appropriate at the time. This is the process of "talking about it". There is a myth around that when someone has problems, simply talking about it helps. But how can it unless something changes as a result. And since the change has to be within the person doing the talking, and talking by itself has no known method of changing constructs, some other process has to occur. That process is one of listening.

Listen to what it is you are doing and saying. Even when the tide is strong, try to take a small step back and listen to yourself as though listening to someone else. Begin to think about what it is you're saying, talking about, perhaps complaining about. Also listen to see whether you are giving your chosen helper any room to help! Even the best of professionals can be overwhelmed by an endless stream from a distressed client. Try slowing yourself down, or even stopping and allow space for both of you to explore what is going on.

(d) Experimenting

By this stage you should have acquired a good working knowledge of yourself and your perceptions as they are. But presumably you have not come to this situation in order to maintain them as they are, you want them to change is some ways. And change demands experimentation with new ways of going about things, or new kinds of approaches, or, at the very least, variations of old methods not previously tried.

Experimentation is at the very heart of personal construct psychology. If you remember our discussion of the metaphor of "person-the-scientist", Kelly pointed out that we were always, continuously, in the business of creating hypotheses about our world, making predictions, *and then testing them out*. Having a prediction which puts limitations upon you but which you are not prepared to test out is useless.

How many times have you stated something in your life as fact, and when asked why you think it, have replied that you simply know it. When faced with the next question, that of how do you know or have you actually tried it out to see, you may become irritable and aggressive, perhaps saying it is not worth it, you know the result already. This insistence with not only making a prediction, but then acting upon it as though it had been tested out is a common fallacy. We all do it at times, usually because we don't want to face the consequences of our experiment. Having said this, of course, we must not be negative. Although we occasionally think we can bypass the need to carry out the experiments our predictions indicate we should, more often than not we do proceed with them. The fact that you are currently reading this book is in itself an experiment. You must have made some predictions about it, or about its contents, before you started. Reading it will be the experiment to find out whether those predictions will be correct or otherwise. Each separate one of you (assuming that more than one person reads this eventually) will have slightly different predictions, and the purpose of your experiments will have different consequences for you. But reading this remains an experiment which you have chosen to carry out.

When you enter therapy, or supervision, or carry out business research, you are automatically embarking on a major experiment. Your prediction, usually, is that the process is going to help you in some way, but at the outset of the experiment you may have no idea how. The implication here is that the outcome of one experiment may lead to new predictions necessitating further experiments. The process is endless.

In therapy, you as client are experimenting with the therapist's ability to help you. As you accept your own role in your life, and explore its meaning, you will begin to discover areas where you have not checked out your predictions thoroughly. You will probably be encouraged to test these out properly. You will probably find areas which seem blocked off, and you will be encouraged to consider alternatives both from your current armoury of constructs and the development of new ones to deal with the problem. These will require experiments. All the exploration, listening, and acceptance does is lead you into understanding your current predictions, understanding how you deal with them, and encouraging you to find new ones and test them out.

Some of these experiments may take place in the environment with your professional adviser. But most of them, especially the most important in your life, take place precisely there—in your life. It is important to remember that you can only try out new or different experiments in the environment about which the predictions are being made. You may be able to rehearse some experiments beforehand, but ultimately there is no substitute for actual reality.

Let us imagine for example that you are having difficulty in relation to one of your parents. There is something you want to tell them, either about them or about yourself. Your prediction is that the response will be very negative, and will leave you feeling hurt and distressed. You may not know how to begin to discuss the matter, and so you never have. Now in this situation nothing will substitute for actually having the discussion with your parent, and ultimately you are going to need to carry out that experiment. But in the context of therapy, it may be possible to try out different ways of approaching the topic to try to reduce the anticipated negative reaction. Perhaps your old methods of initiating important conversations have to some extent invited a rejecting response. You can be encouraged to practise alternatives with your therapist first, then perhaps with sympathetic friends, before finally trying out the main problem. Although the focus of any work you as client do is related to your world, you do not have to rush out and experiment in a headlong or headstrong manner. You, together with your professional, can temper the experiments to a manageable progression, one that reduces the development of threat, and increases the chances of positive validation.

We could probably write an entire book on the subject of experimentation alone. That is clearly not practicable or desirable here. What is important is to underline the value of being prepared to try out something different, or something new, in approaching whatever problems you may have. Even when you may feel that a particular idea is hopeless, it may be worth testing it out. Until you do, you don't *know* whether it will work or not. You will find examples of our clients' experiments throughout the book. Finally, and briefly, we want to mention a particular extreme form of experiment outlined by Kelly. This is known as "fixed role therapy". This is more fully described elsewhere (Chapter 10) but bears an outline here. Where major change in constructs is indicated it may be more economical to start building a new set of constructs to replace the old altogether. In this case, the first step is to build up a detailed picture of the client's construct system. Then, usually in conjunction with a group of professionals, an alternative set of constructs is put together. These new constructs are separate from the old ones, based on neither emergent or contrast poles. A written picture of how the client would be if he held these constructs is drawn up and presented to the client. If you, as client, can make sense of this new perspective, then you would be asked to go away and enact this person in your day-to-day life.

Now obviously this is a major undertaking for both client and professional, and in its pure, large-scale form is seldom undertaken. But it does serve to illustrate that the process of experimentation can be done in broad sweeps as well as small details, and that sometimes broad sweeps may help more radical change as a result. A modified form of fixed role therapy (Fran) is described in Chapter 10.

(e) Learning

This is the final part of what you, as client, have to do. Learning is not perhaps the best word as it tends to have connotations of learning theory, or stimulus–response psychology which is not what is desired here.

Learning in the PCP context is that of incorporating into your construct system the results of the experiments you have carried out. Your predictions lead you to carry out experiments either to validate or to invalidate those predictions. You want to know whether what you are trying out works or not. It is therefore incumbent upon you to look at the result of your experiment and review your predictions accordingly.

Thus the development of new experiments carries with it the implication that new results will be obtained, and those new results will lead to an alteration in the current construct system. Whatever client role you have undertaken, you will be encouraged to try some things differently from how you have approached them before. These suggestions will not come in a vacuum, or from a distant professional with no apparent relevance to you. They will be made on the basis of the joint exploration of your current constructs, and a joint understanding of where they, and your system, is letting you down or causing problems. You should be keen to try out these experiments, and certainly keen to learn from them, even if only to prove a prediction you have always held but never tested! Of course, as with any experiments, some will not work out. Invalidation of predictions is at least as valuable as validation. Continuous invalidation, though, is an extremely depressing experience even though recognition of such a state should tell you something about your predictions. But don't give up trying if you do not always get the answer you want, and don't try to fix the evidence either. Trying repeatedly to force the answer you want out of circumstances which are clearly not giving it is a route to disaster. You may remember that this kind of action is called "hostility".

We have outlined above five main areas which you as client would be expected to do. Of course, these apply to all of us all the time. We should all be doing these as we move through our lives. Normally we are not particularly conscious of the process, and whatever situation you are in, you need to become conscious of it, and actively participate in it.

THE PROFESSIONAL'S PERSPECTIVE

As a PCP professional, in whatever capacity, you have two overlapping areas to cover. The first of these is to be "a professional" with all that that term implies. The second is specifically to be a PCP professional which imposes particular activities upon the generality of being a professional.

(a) Being a Professional

It may seem unnecessary to outline some of the issues that follow because any self-respecting professional would assume their existence. But we have already indicated that assumptions that are not checked out may lead to the realisation considerably farther on that the self-same assumptions are not shared by others around you! The safest attitude is assume nothing without checking it out. Then you should know where you are at. A further point is that this book is being written for professionals *and* clients. While all professionals may agree about what being a professional is about, many clients have only a very hazy idea. So while this section is principally for you professionals, potential clients will also read it to find out what you are expected to do too!

Having said this it is not our intention to devote long paragraphs expounding the details of such issues as ethics, training, supervision, peer-group review, audit or whatever. Nor would we attempt to lay down rules on dress, environment or general behaviour. Different professionals interpret the broad canvas in their own individual ways as indeed they should. Being a professional should not be a straitjacket with totally rigid structures defining all aspects of contact with clients. Clients themselves need a variety of professionals to choose from, not a collection of identical clones.

There are two areas of generality which do require to be mentioned. These are ethics and training. Most professional organisations require as a precursor to being able to claim entry to that profession a set training procedure, and the acceptance of a set of ethics applying to that profession. This is true of all the major "caring" professions, such as medicine, nursing, clinical psychology, occupational therapy, and speech therapy. Each of these incorporates some aspects of counselling into their training, some more than others, and each subscribes to a well-tested code of ethics. Similarly, organisations relating to business or management have similar, though obviously different, training programmes, and codes of ethics specifically appropriate for their field of operation. Most, if not all, PCP counsellors, or PCP "experts" in their field belong to one of these organisations already, and since PCP would see itself as only one tool in an armoury of possibilities, this is how it should be.

Specific training in PCP comes from a variety of resources, some relatively informal such as "in-house" courses, special interest groups and so forth, and others much more formal like the diploma courses offered by the Centre for Personal Construct Psychology in London. In all these situations, the basic training of the primary profession, and its ethical code remains in force while carrying out any activity under the PCP aegis. This is important to remember for both professional *and* client.

(b) Being a PCP Professional

We have already made the point above that all those matters which apply to being a professional in general, also apply to those professionals applying PCP. However, there are a number of particular points which need re-emphasising at this time about what makes a PCP professional different from professionals applying other theoretical approaches. We want to cover the following areas: subsuming, assisting change, and suspension of own constructs. We are not about to begin another discussion on reflexivity, although it permeates all the activities of a PCP professional, and offers a realistic substitute to compulsory personal therapy in training. Nor do we feel it necessary to cover again the techniques outlined in the previous chapter for the client to expect. It is assumed that anyone wishing to consider themselves a PCP professional will acquaint themselves to the appropriate degree with the theory and literature pertaining to their field of interest, and will learn to apply the techniques effectively. In other words, it is the professional's own responsibility to ensure he or she is adequately trained to perform the tasks expected.

(1) Subsuming

This is probably the most important aspect for you as a professional to grasp hold of. It is the process by which you can make a "diagnosis" of the problem with which you are presented, and a guide for your attempts to assist change in your client. It is a tenet of PCP that before you make attempts to help your client change you have a working model in your head of the way your client views his or her world. Of course, it is impossible to say that the process of obtaining such a view does not itself promote some change—any interaction consists of checking out some predictions on both sides and may therefore lead to minor construct system alterations. But it is important to remember that before you leap in to "help" your client, you need to understand what is actually happening psychologically inside them. Although this may sound self-evident, the necessity to subsume your client's construct system *before* proceeding to promote or assist change does separate PCP from many other approaches where the understanding of the client goes hand in hand with the provision of interpretations or the promotion of change. The word "diagnosis" has unfortunate medical connotations but still remains the most useful one to describe what happens. You need to identify the problem, and what is causing it, before you can possibly know how to go about helping with it, or "treating" it to pursue the metaphor.

Subsuming is about being able to see the world through the eyes of your client. It is about exploring with your client their system of predictions; their system of constructs; and their difficulties in applying them effectively. Subsuming demands that you make no assumptions about what your client means. It involves continual checking out that you understand *your client's* meanings. It is about exploring *with* your client their perceptions, fears, and concerns, without prejudice, without putting them at a disadvantage by appearing to understand them better than they do themselves. As Kelly himself said, when you don't know something, ask the client, he or she may tell you. After all, the client is the expert on the client. You are the expert on PCP. Together, by sharing your respective information, you may be able to achieve something which apart does not work.

Subsuming is also something of a privilege for any professional. Think about how well you know your friends, or even your partners. Your client is allowing you to explore the furthermost reaches of the way they make sense of their world. It is an extremely personal and intimate experience. It therefore goes without saying—or at least, ought to go without needing to be said—that the permission you receive to proceed carries with it the requirements to be understanding when your client becomes anxious or threatened by the process, to be sympathetic without being sycophantic, to be compassionate, and above all, to remember that you are human too.

(2) Assisting change

Since your client has presented with a problem with which help is requested, merely making a "diagnosis" is not usually enough. There may be some situations in which once the client understands the cause of the problem for himself, he can then go away and do something about it on his own. But in most cases, your client may understand the point you have jointly reached, but remain rather at a loss as to what to do about it.

This is the point at which your function to assist change comes into action.

Note that the word used is to *assist* change. It is not your function to tell your client how to be, or what constructs to keep or discard like teaching them to play cards. You are not there to provide "advice", good or otherwise. Your role is one of assistance, almost that of a catalyst, encouraging reactions in your client without imposing anything of yourself into the reaction. (See "Suspending your own constructs" below.) We have already looked at the clients' role in this activity under a discussion of experimentation. Obviously while it is your clients' responsibility to be prepared to try out new experiments, they need some help in devising them, and feeling safe in carrying them out. You, armed with your understanding of your client's personal system, and with your general understanding of PCP, should be able to help your client see new paths to try out, and help him or her evaluate the results. Evaluation of the outcomes is, of course, at least as important as doing the experiments themselves. Unless the results are examined in the light of the predictions underlying the experiment, then neither validation or invalidation of those predictions will take place.

Other areas of assisting change may be to encourage loosening or tightening of the system, either in part or as a whole. This process, discussed together with "The creativity cycle" in Chapter 4, also leads to new kinds of experiments as the cycle develops.

Change does involve not only the development of new constructs, but also using the personal construct system differently. Encouragement to use the creativity cycle as mentioned above is one area of change. Others include examination of the types of construct used—whether pre-emptive, constellatory or propositional and whether these are appropriate in the context. And so forth and so on. This is not the place to examine in detail a whole range of different "diagnoses", and the areas involved in assisting change. Suffice it to say that both subsuming and assisting change require a detailed and comfortable knowledge of PCP. Otherwise it is like the blind leading the blind!

(3) Suspending your own constructs

In many ways the ability to suspend your own construct system while working with that of your client is one of the hardest techniques to learn. After all, your construct system as a whole is what makes your personality. It is what you use for predicting relationships, events and activities. Yet here you are, facing your client, being asked to suspend yourself effectively.

In some senses, it is impossible to achieve total suspension. The way you have dressed on a particular morning is itself an external manifestation of your construing. Where and how you sit in an interview, together with a whole collection of personal mannerisms, may give clues to your client if he or she is observant enough to notice them.

There are, however, two aspects of suspending your own constructs that bear special mention. First is the point that one of the important matters in training in PCP is using the reflexivity to examine your own presentation to a potential client. No-one is ever going to understand themselves wholly, but it is important to recognise the more major kinds of responses you are likely to make to the information a client presents you with. As your training progresses and you have increasingly detailed supervision as part of the training, so your own role in the interaction will come under scrutiny, and you will be expected to apply the same rigour to your actions and responses as to those of your client. Your own self-knowledge is important to know how to keep your own judgements, and constructs, out of the professional milieu.

The second point is to be aware of your assumptions. The assumption that your client shares some of your aspirations, cultural beliefs, ways of dealing with situations or whatever is extremely easily made. We all operate on assumptions about other people and it requires a great deal of training and self-discipline to get out of the majority of the habit. It is so easy to think that you and your client see things similarly, or that what has worked for you will work for them. Indeed, they might on occasion, but you cannot assume that. In order genuinely to see the world through your client's construct system, you have to put yours on one side.

The one exception to this process is your collection of professional constructs. You need to retain your training, your ethics, and your professional knowledge of how a personal construct system works, and be able to continue to use all these. What is suspended is your personal construing, as least so far as you are able. This process always keeps you on your toes, and is one of the reasons we believe you should always have supervision, however experienced you may have become.

9

CAN I DO IT BY MYSELF?

Yes, but....

It might be better to consider the question as "Can I do it for myself?" We have already discussed in some detail the whole issue of reflexivity, the idea that the psychological processes apply to each and every one of us. It therefore follows that a professional and a client are not necessary to elucidate these processes. Because they are unique and personal, they exist in each individual, and are therefore accessible within each individual. So the theory, with its emphasis on reflexivity, says that you ought to be able to do it by yourself.

The next question is of course "What am I able to do by myself?" And this is where the "but..." comes in. Essentially, to what extent can one person, without outside help, carry out all the functions outlined in the last two chapters—and carry them out honestly, rigorously and effectively.

Much depends on what you are trying to achieve. For the average person, a good working knowledge of PCP may well help them to explore and understand their own personal construct system better. In turn this may make some decision-making easier, or the directions to choose more clear. Having a generally effective and smooth-running system to begin with does make the exploration easier. On the other hand, if you feel as though you are in real difficulties, feeling very anxious and threatened, and perhaps pretty desperate, then trying to do all the repair work by yourself is probably asking too much of yourself.

In essence, if treatment is required because the system is breaking down or has broken down, then you probably need some outside help, and to assume you can self-help on your own from learning about PCP is unrealistic. If, on the other hand, you want to understand yourself better, or to explore a particular subsystem, or to anticipate possible problems in the future, then a good working knowledge of PCP may well be good preventive psychology. It is better to avoid crises altogether than have to sort the problems out in them. So if you want to use PCP as a kind of psychological prophylaxis then you are welcome to try.

One further matter needs to be mentioned here before discussing in greater depth how you may be able to use PCP for yourself. You have already seen how powerful some of the techniques are for finding out how people see their personal worlds. The process of eliciting, laddering and pyramiding constructs provides rapid entry into the intimately personal world of the individual. In therapy, or other client/professional relationship, specific permission is granted to allow the professional to explore in this way, and the client is protected by the professionalism of his helper. It is, however, very tempting to use some of these techniques outside the strict client/professional relationship. One of us found ourself some years ago at a dinner party becoming increasingly frustrated at not being able to make sense of what one of the other guests was elaborating politically. Almost without thinking about it, some constructs were elicited in the conversation over the dinner table, and a process of laddering begun. And although it rapidly became much clearer, not only what that particular guest really did mean, but also why it was important for him to hold those beliefs, the guest was both amazed and appalled to discover himself suddenly being led into making highly personal statements in the middle of a dinner without really realising how he had got there. Most of the rest of the guests seemed to feel embarrassed at becoming the recipients of such personal material.

The purpose of this story is to wave a cautionary finger. Apply PCP to yourself for your own exploration and understanding by all means. You give yourself permission. Also, by all means use your knowledge to help you listen to others, and avoid making assumptions about them. But do not use it to start probing their personal systems without some form of clear permission from them first. To return to the dinner mentioned above, had some conversation asking for clarification of the remarks prefaced the elicitation and laddering, together with an open explanation of what was happening, and a clear statement that the guest could say stop whenever he wanted, much anguish might have been avoided. The moral is: be careful. PCP is a powerful theory, and like all powerful items, can be mishandled. Remember you need permission to use it on anyone else.

USING IT ON YOURSELF

There are two circumstances in which using PCP on yourself may be valuable and helpful. The first is when you are faced with a specific problem or decision which, for some reason you do not fully understand, you seem unable to resolve. Here the problem is focused, and you have a clear goal in mind. You want to explore this area in order to resolve your apparent confusion. The second circumstance is the much more general one of simply wanting to know more about yourself, of beginning to understand yourself better, and of beginning to use the idea of reflexivity to the full by actually seeing yourself in PCP terms. Whichever your objective, specific or general, many of the procedures will be similar, and have been described previously. Those that have will only be mentioned again here, with the exception of the self-characterisation. The principles of operating PCP, as we have repeated endlessly, apply to everyone equally, and so there is no fundamental difference in applying it to yourself than in applying it to someone else. In fact, the only real difference is that you have to hold on to the professional constructs while at the same time exploring your own construct system. This obviously can pose some problems on occasions, especially if what you are trying to explore is sensitive or threatening. At least, in those circumstances, you are in a good position to give yourself permission to stop!

Understanding Specific Problems

It is perhaps worth stating at the outset here that the division of problems into specific and general is rather arbitrary. Your construct system is interlinked, and so investigation of one part almost inevitably touches upon other areas. This can lead to a kind of knock-on effect whereby you never seem to reach an end of related constructs until you have moved so far away from the original issue that you are thoroughly confused. If you want to explore a particular issue you have to be disciplined enough to stay with that issue alone and not allow yourself to be sidetracked into other, often more interesting or less threatening, areas. This is, of course, one reason why it is harder to do this on your own than with a therapist/counsellor, but it is by no means impossible.

At this stage we were going to provide a hypothetical example of how someone goes about exploring one of their own issues. But we immediately ran into two problems. The first was that, by the nature of the activity, it is only done by one person, alone. We could not draw on the experiences we have of working with people because that is precisely what we are not talking about here. The only alternative was for one of us to provide an example from our own lives, and, quite frankly, neither of us felt that we wanted to do that. After all, the desire to explore something on one's own probably has to do in part with wanting to keep it, and the results, to oneself. It is a private process, and should remain so unless you yourself wish to make it more public.

The second problem was that even when we tried to find a hypothetical problem, the variety of possibilities was so great as to require quite different explorations for each of them. Where a problem related to interpersonal difficulties, for example, the exploration might involve elicitation of constructs from amongst people you know, with some laddering and pyramiding particularly focused on the person, or situation, in which the difficulties are experienced. Conversely, if you are having great difficulty in choosing between two alternatives, Finn Tschudi's ABC model (see below) may be a useful starting point. The point to be made here is that, as in joint or group work with PCP, the actual approach has to be tailored to the personal and unique position presented by the client. In this instance, as you are the client and the professional, you have to do the tailoring for yourself. This may involve some trial and error but this itself is no bad thing as it may encourage you to look in ways that throw up unexpected results.

Given that we have not been able to give you a hypothetical example, what can we do to help you? For one thing, we can provide you with some encouragement to try something out for yourself. Why not sit down at this point and think of a small, but maybe niggling, problem in your own life. The chances are that you are on your own at the moment—reading tends to be a fairly solitary activity, and you can do this in your head if you want to. Don't choose something of huge significance in your life. You want something you can begin to play with at this stage. Once you have thought of the "problem" just begin to think of how you might go about exploring your constructs about it. Remember that all constructs have two poles, so if your problem generates a particular idea, try thinking of its contrast. This gives you a basis for either laddering or pyramiding. Begin to build up a picture of the constructs that are involved. If you have a pen and paper at hand, write some of them down. It is always easier if laddering or pyramiding constructs to have a written record. It also makes it easier to see what you have found rather than trying to keep it all in your head. Depending on what your problem is—a person, a situation, an activity or whatever, try to think of other similar but different equivalents. Other people who don't provoke the problem response, other situations where you feel at ease rather than under stress, other activities you enjoy rather than feel forced to do. Use these contrasts to elaborate how you construe amongst them together with the one causing the problem.

By this time you should already have quite a group of constructs available to tell you something about your views of your problem. We mentioned above, however, a particular technique outlined by Finn Tschudi (39) which he called the ABC-model. This model is useful in exploring the reasons behind not moving from one pole of a construct to another apparently more attractive one, or for examining difficulties in making a decision between two alternatives.

In this model, A defines the dimension along which you want to move. You find yourself at **a1** and wish to move to **a2**. For example you may see yourself as "depressed" and wish to see yourself as "not being depressed". Tschudi, quoting Greenwald, then asks why a person apparently wanting to move along this axis in fact does not. Here he points out that the problem (**a1**) has payoffs for the person concerned, that it has advantages in the here and now. So the next step is to ask for advantages and disadvantages of both **a1** and **a2**. The advantages of **a2** and the disadvantages of **a1** from the B axis. This is the axis showing why you want to move along A. Where you are at has disadvantages (**b1**) while where you want to move to has advantages (**b2**). The third stage is based on the notion that the problem has some positive implications, while the desired alternative has some negative ones. This is the C axis, and is the construct or group of constructs which keep you from moving, what Dennis Hinkle has called an "implicative dilemma". Thus **c2** are the positive implications of the problem **a1** while **c1** are the negative implications of the apparently desirable alternative.

Tschudi quotes an example based on the *"being depressed"* vs *"not being depressed"* axis which shows how the system works:

a1	being depressed		**a2**	not being depressed
b1	1. I can't do things I'd like to		**b2**	1. I could do things I like
	2. I'm not as good a wife as I would like to be			2. I could be a better wife
	3. I pity my husband who is so much alone			3. I could keep my husband more company
c1	1. must do unwanted things		**c2**	1. avoid doing unwanted things
	2. must play happy wife—is disliked			2. avoid playing happy wife which I am not
	3. must have intercourse when not wanting to			3. avoid unwanted intercourse

This example clearly shows how the model works, and makes rather more sense of the client's difficulty in doing what she apparently wants, which is to become "not depressed". The implications for her of such movement may be more dreadful than those of remaining depressed—in fact, as Hinkle said, an implicative dilemma.

The model can be extrapolated to help look at difficult decisions, where the A axis is the two alternatives. The process is the same—examining the advantages and disadvantages for *you* of making either choice. In this situation what may become clear is not so much why one choice is better than the other, but why you find it so difficult to make either. Each may have such positive or negative implications as to make any movement impossible. While such knowledge does not instantly resolve the conflict, it does make you aware of what the issues are, and gives you an opportunity to go on and explore them in more depth.

Remember that if you are having difficulty experimenting with your "problem", whatever you have chosen, that this is probably the first time you have tried using PCP on your own, and perhaps even the first time you have tried some of the techniques. Like any skill, it takes some practice to get better at it, so don't expect to be able to resolve everything all at once. If it were that easy, no-one would have any problems or difficulties at all!

Understanding Yourself Generally

In some ways this process is easier than trying to explore a specific problem. There is less urgency, and more sense of wanting to explore for the sake of exploration and understanding than to achieve any particular outcome. In fact this can be likened to playing with PCP. Some people may regard the idea of playing with a serious psychological theory as being rather heretical. They would argue that it should be treated with the respect it deserves. It is not there for enjoyment, but should only be left in the hands of experts and used in *proper* circumstances. This seems to us an extremely restrictive and rather negative view of Kelly's theory, and not one which we believe he would have espoused.

Play is used as a method of learning. Children at play are discovering things about their world even as they are enjoying themselves. Some of the most popular and enduring toys are those which maintain the interest of the child long past the initial surprise and pleasure. Play is about exploration and discovery, and about imagination and fantasy. It is about learning and prediction, but simultaneously about discovering other ways of seeing the world. Above all play is important not only for children but also for adults as a method of loosening tightly held constructs, and trying out new ones, in a circumstance which allows less "responsible" behaviour.

So how does this relate to using PCP for yourself generally? The answer is that you can use it as a plaything to explore yourself. Admittedly you have to remember that it is a powerful and sophisticated toy, but the process of using it can be exciting, enjoyable, fun and interesting, along with producing serious information and giving you new insight into yourself. There is such a variety of options. You can set yourself the task of writing a self-characterisation for a start—often an extremely useful beginning to discover what you think of yourself. You can examine some of your beliefs and ideas, look at why you choose and wear the clothes you do, or examine who you feel attracted to and what the differences are between those you are and those you are not. The range of possibilities is endless, and the process is fascinating. After all, what you are exploring is your *personal* view of the world. What could be more interesting to you?

CAN IT BE DANGEROUS?

Initially, when we conceived the idea of writing this book, we intended to have a whole chapter devoted to the question of whether PCP could be dangerous. The decision not to was taken for two main reasons. The first was that we felt that having a whole chapter devoted to "dangerousness" vastly over-emphasised an issue that certainly needed to be mentioned, but not to that extent. Any psychological theory mishandled can be "dangerous" but this one is no more so than any other, and indeed could be argued to be less so than some. The emphasis on the *personal*, the insistence on its *reflexivity*, the demand that work is done in *partnership*, all combine to provide unique safety features either for a client, or for yourself working alone. We believe that, correctly handled, it is a powerful theory of understanding of personality, but that it has built-in safeguards which render it focused in its effects rather than some more blunderbuss approaches.

The second main reason was that we felt a whole chapter with "dangerous" in the title might well prove frightening, anxiety-provoking or even threatening to some readers. After all, we have just been discussing you playing with this theory, and you might have felt concerned about this apparent irresponsibility with a chapter on dangerousness just over the page. You would hardly feel encouraged to play if you anticipated it might explode in your face.

You might well be asking by now why we have included even a section on dangerousness. The answer here is because there are circumstances in which its misuse can cause problems rather than resolve them, although dangerousness is probably an over-dramatic word to use. One area, for example, was outlined in discussing the use of the theory and its techniques on someone else without having the appropriate permission to do so. As stated then, it is very effective at looking for the personal core of a person's beliefs and approach to life. Each of us has the right to have our privacy respected, and our psychological worlds are about as private as anything can be. Such a misuse can be dangerous either because it may ruin friendships or spoil social occasions, or, and more seriously, it may evoke areas of sensitivity or threat which it is not possible to handle in the context at the time.

A second area of caution is in the attempts to use PCP for yourself. Remember that you need to know what you are doing. Effective use of PCP does require good understanding and knowledge of the theory and its techniques, and this book only attempts to provide an introduction to these. You should not go away after reading this assuming that you can tackle any problem with confidence. You may well have started on the road to being able to do so, but personality is a vastly complex issue, and no exploration should be undertaken lightly. Furthermore, although we would encourage you to play with the theory for yourselves, this should not be seen as an alternative to seeking expert help when problems become too large or difficult to deal with on your own. This is not do-it-yourself psychology which obviates the need for specialist help. But it may provide a framework in which such help can be sought and accepted.

Finally, this approach should not in our view be used as a justification for any actions you take on the grounds that they are part of your *personal* system, and if they don't fit in with those around you, hard luck. Each of us as individuals operates in society, and accepts varying degrees of sociality and commonality as a result. A whole society of individuals operating with no regard to others' construing would reach anarchy very rapidly. Although this theory emphasises your personal view of the world, this does not mean that you should focus on that to the exclusion of trying to understand other peoples' views of their worlds, in order to be able to live, breathe and have your being alongside them. It is not a prescription for selfishness, and such a construal would be dangerous for yourself and others around you.

10

HOW WILL IT ALL END?

HOW LONG WILL IT TAKE?

All clients come to therapy with expectations, however vague, as we have said. But there is usually much anxiety—much outside the range of their construing. So there will be questions, even if they are too uncertain to ask them during the first meeting. The therapist will always try to encourage people to voice them and express any doubts, though these may not be forthcoming until later. Perhaps the most recurrent, and one of the most difficult to answer, is "How long will it take?" This is a very reasonable question, particularly if the person is without experience of therapy and has some notion in mind of "a course of treatment". If therapy is anticipated as something the therapist "does" to you according to a programme he or she has worked out, then it should be possible to say how long it will take. It will be clear, though, that PCP *has* no programme and that it depends largely on what the client brings and what we make of it together as to how long the process will take.

Brief Encounters

We referred in Chapter 6 to a therapist's complaint early on in a course she was taking that she seldom had a great deal of time with any one client and therefore many of the "techniques" were irrelevant. She reconstrued as we saw and found ways of her own of listening credulously and picking up people's themes without all the methods we have described for eliciting constructs, setting up grids and so on. In the same chapter we described briefly some of the ways in which Tom Ravenette works with children, sometimes having only one meeting with them. Others, offering careers advice, for example, may also have only one or perhaps two sessions with their clients and still are able to pull out important issues at stake and give them something significant to take away with them.

This can happen in many situations. Where there is an important decision to make, for example, one session can sometimes be enough for the person to go away ready to take action. A young woman came to discuss her "indecision" about whether to start a family or take a new and important step in her career. Using the CPC cycle as a basis we set out all the factors involved for her:

A. Circumspection

The issues to be considered:

> Her age (she was 33)
> Her wish to have a child at some point
> Her husband's wish for a child
> Her mother's pressure on her to have a child
> Her waning ambition with regard to work
> Earning no money
> Her husband's good salary
> Her wish for real change

As she looked at these points and talked around them she realised two things. Her mother's pressure was arousing in her old resentments about having decisions made for her when she was younger and therefore she was partly undecided about having a baby now because her mother was pushing her. Her "wish for real change" was more comprehensive than she realised and she saw it as closely linked with her waning ambition with regard to work. She did want a new role. So— should this be a new work role or a role as a mother? How important, also, was her husband's wish? Very. And underneath it all was her fear that she might not actually make a very good mother. This was undoubtedly the strongest factor of all although she had not listed it at first.

B. Pre-emption

On the issue of being a mother

The rest of the session was spent in helping her to elaborate what she thought a good mother should be and what qualities she already had or could develop. She left saying that she would talk to her husband again, not say a word to her mother, and let me know what she had decided.

C. Control

She decided to start a family

In another instance a couple came twice. They had had a good marriage for a number of years but lately had found themselves quarrelling quite bitterly. They wondered whether they should think about splitting up before one of them did damage to the other. We looked first at what had been good about their relationship and the life they led and it was clear that they valued the same things. Then we looked at what had changed in the last year or so. They began by saying that each other had changed and there was no doubt that their behaviour when they had been together had—in ways which neither of them could ever have imagined. When asked about their circumstances, however, a number of important things emerged. First, they were working together every day instead of sometimes together and sometimes separately. This gave them a feeling of having "no space" and each felt they were seeing too little of other people. Secondly, they were both working overtime in order to pay for a new home and were exhausted.

They agreed that it was perfectly possible to work separately again (they were cabin crew for an airline and could ask for simultaneous flights rather than the same flight). Also they questioned whether there was such a hurry to move house. They both liked the one they lived in now, but had wanted something "better". They decided there and then to stop the overtime and as soon as possible have a holiday. They also agreed to a number of experiments to try to break the pattern of quarrelling. First, they would "believe each other". This not only meant believing in stated facts but accepting that the meaning of what the other said was true for him or her. Then they would "stop the old tapes". If they were aware of bringing up old complaints or criticisms they would "take them as read". Finally, they would really try to listen to each other, whatever was going on.

Although this couple were exhausted and very angry with each other at this point, they did seem to want to sort things out and to understand something of how they had come to this situation. It seemed fair to predict that the practical changes would help a good deal and they appeared likely to attempt the experiments. They delayed their second session because they found themselves able to have a holiday sooner than they thought. When they returned things were improved. They were on different flights which more or less coincided so that their free time could be spent together. And they had stopped the overtime. The holiday had restored them and they were both more hopeful. They expressed no doubt now about staying together but were anxious that nothing like it should ever happen again. We spent some time predicting future events which might prove difficult and looking at ways in which they might approach them. The crucial element seemed to be to continue to "listen" to each other and accept, if not share, each other's meanings.

There are no miracles of course and it will be clear that these two instances concerned people at moments of crisis who were otherwise able to function well. They did not need therapy as such. Only the opportunity to talk through a problem with someone who could offer them, without "judgement", some structure at a time of difficulty. There are many other examples of where this approach can help in one or two sessions and it is being used by social workers, educationalists, counsellors and others in this way.

The Therapeutic Series

Where a series of sessions is likely, however, it is usual to come to an agreement during the first meeting on a number of initial sessions to explore the problem in some depth. Only after this period of, say, four to six sessions should it be possible to give some indication of the duration of therapy, at least in broad terms. It should have become clear by then whether what needs to be worked on together is a problem related more to the client's difficulty with current circumstances or something with a "history" and complexity which has troubled them for a long time. The client's general way of managing life and some aspects of the construing system as a whole should have emerged, indicating what resources are there, how strong the structure of the personality or how frail it might be and threatened by change. These and other factors will lead the therapist to predict a relatively short period of therapy or to suggest the need to plan for a longer term. There may be the option for the client to settle for tackling more immediate issues, even where there seems to be a good deal else to work through. It must be their choice, although it is the therapist's responsibility to put the alternatives as he or she sees them clearly and honestly. Occasionally there *is* only a limited time, though not as limited as the brief encounters just described. The client will only be around for a few weeks or months, perhaps. Even if both realise that there is much that could be done given a longer period it should always be possible to do something to ease the immediate crisis and give the client something to take away to work with. Here again, clarity of aims is crucial—what you are intending to attempt together and what you are deliberately leaving for the time being at least. Most therapists and clients prefer to work consistently and regularly but, because of the client's work, perhaps, this is not always possible. Someone who travels abroad frequently, for example, may find it impossible to agree to a regular time and it is important for the therapist to be willing to adjust to this. We have found this difficult, but not insuperable. It is harder for the therapist to plan a course of action or predict the outcome of experiments with a gap of weeks between sessions. So a different way of working must be found where broad aims are established and alternative ways of carrying them out evolved for the client to pursue according to time and circumstances. Some form of correspondence may supplement meetings or the client can keep and perhaps send a "diary" to the therapist. It asks a lot of both parties but can be very fruitful.

After a series of meetings therapist and client may feel that a break is appropriate. If a good deal of ground has been covered, it may be useful for the client to stop for a while to assimilate what he or she has understood, to experiment with changes. This can be much more productive than plodding on regardless just because there is more to do. Another variation comes about when the client is focusing on a particular area which could be helped by some approach such as yoga, physical treatment, a course to enhance some skill or introduce a new dimension into his or her life. Therapy can go on concurrently, of course, but sometimes a break will be helpful. What is important in all this is that client and therapist should have some plan in mind in relation to time as well as the aims involved and not simply meet regularly, as if that in itself will do the trick. Plans should be modified as new material emerges, but there should always be a sense of purpose and therapy should never just peter out.

HOW DOES IT TURN OUT?

This is an even more difficult question to answer than the one about duration. It should be clear from earlier chapters that the processes begun in therapy never "end". If the aim is reconstruction and the development of a creative approach to life, therapy will only be the starting point to the venture. But, as we know, clients naturally have expectations and concerns about the outcome of therapy and it is important for the therapist to understand the first and appreciate the second. If expectations are for some kind of magic "cure" of all the clients' ills it will be part of the therapist's job to help them to view their situation differently. Coming to accept responsibility for your own change, we have said, can be threatening at first— liberating in the long run.

The most helpful method of showing the various ways that therapy might turn out in different circumstances seems to us to be through examples. We can only present a few here, but we hope they will at least give some idea of the many possible outcomes and the factors which govern their similarities and differences. We shall also refer you later to other case studies to be found in the PCP literature. Since we are equally concerned with helping children and their families as with helping adults, we shall begin with a study of a child.

Henry

The problems—the people

At the age of seven Henry had a severe stutter and had not responded to behavioural treatment. His mother was very anxious for his future and his father, who had stammered himself as a boy, hated the idea of therapy and declared that "the little blighter will grow out of it". This disagreement between the parents was something of a stumbling-block for a while and it was some time before the father would consent to discuss it and agreed to a meeting. He believed that his wife spoiled their only son, who was born when they were in their forties and, an ex-policeman himself, he couldn't bear any sign of "weakness". The mother, Marion, was rather timid and apologetic and clearly quite frightened of her husband. Nevertheless, she dug her heels in and brought her son along.

At first, Henry said very little and eyed me suspiciously. He hadn't liked his former therapist and hated the work he did with her. We negotiated six sessions, during which we would not only experiment to find the most useful way of "smoothing his speech down" but to give me a chance to get to know them and they to see whether they were comfortable with me. Speech work, which focused mainly on slowing the rate and aiming for a natural smoothness continued parallel with PCP procedures and within six months Henry was fluent in many situations which enabled us to work on other aspects of communication and relationship which had been affected by his stammering. Here I shall concentrate only on the PCP aspects of what I did.

During those early sessions, among other things, Henry completed a rated grid, which Marion then filled in as if she were her son. This was to see how well she was able to see things through his eyes and she was quite happy to do this. Figures 10.1 and 10.2 show their two versions. Let us look at

'Henry'

1 ——→ 3 ——→ 5

		Mummy	Daddy	Denny (best friend)	Barry	Me as I am now	Derek	Tim (cousin)	Aunt Edna	Mrs Peecher	Miss Robins	Terry	Me as I'd like to be
1	strong / weak	3	4	1	3	4	2	1	4	3	3	3	1
2	nice / nasty	1	1	1	1	3	5	1	1	4	1	2	3
3	funny / serious	3	4	1	1	3	1	3	5	5	1	3	1
4	likes to fight back / doesn't fight back	1	1	3	2	2	1	2	1	1	1	1	1
5	kind / helpful / unkind	1	4	3	1	3	5	3	1	3	3	3	1
6	happy / sad	3	3	3	2	3	3	2	3	3	2	3	1
7	not naughty or silly / naughty and silly	1	1	2	1	2	5	2	1	1	2	3	1
8	gives me nice things / doesn't give me things	3	2	4	3	4	5	3	2	2	2	3	3
9	not strict / strict	2	3	–	–	2	–	–	3	2	2	–	5
10	I talk well with.... / I don't talk so well with....	2	3	3	2	5	3	3	3	1	3	3	1
11	has courage, brave / a coward, scared	3	1	2	3	3	2	2	2	3	3	2	1

Figure 10.1 Henry's grid

'Henry' by 'Marion'

1 ——— 3 ——— 5

			Mummy	Daddy	Denny (best friend)	Barny *	Me as I am now	Derek	Tim (cousin)	Aunt Edna	Mrs Peecher	Miss Robins	Terry *	Me as I'd like to be
1	strong	weak	3	1	2	1	2	1	2	1	3	3		1
2	nice	nasty	1	2	1	3	3	4	1	2	4	3		1
3	funny	serious	3	2	3	3	3	1	2	4	4	3		3
4	likes to fight back	doesn't fight back	4	1	3	1	1	1	1	5	5	3		1
5	kind / helpful	unkind	1	2	1	4	2	4	1	1	4	3		1
6	happy	sad	3	2	1	3	3	2	1	3	3	3		1
7	not naughty or silly	naughty and silly	1	1	1	3	2	5	1	1	1	1		1
8	gives me nice things	doesn't give me things	1	1	3	5	3	3	3	1	5	5		3
9	not strict	strict	4	4	3	3	3	3	3	1	5	3		3
10	I talk well with.....	I don't talk so well with.....	2	2	2	3	3	2	2	1	3	3		3
11	has courage, brave	a coward, scared	3	1	2	1	2	1	1	3	3	3		1

Notes from Marion.
* Barny has fallen out of favour since Henry did his rating!
* I have not heard of this one!

Figure 10.2   Marion's grid on Henry

Henry's first. The elements he chose were his parents, his best friend, two other boys in his class, one of whom he disliked, his five-year-old cousin, Tim, his aunt and two teachers, one of whom he liked and the other he didn't. He also rated "Me as I am now" and "Me as I'd like to be". He seemed to enjoy a great sense of potency as he filled in the numbers!

The constructs were elicited by asking him to compare two of the people at a time with one another. He clearly shared his father's emphasis on strength and weakness, which also formed part of a structured conversation we had at one stage. (This is a procedure suggested by Tom Ravenette, where the therapist introduces leading statements for the child to pick up.) He had been talking about fighting and had just said that if any girl beat him in a fight he'd "bash her head in!"

THERAPIST: You're strong are you?
HENRY: Not really very strong. People say I'm quite weak.
THERAPIST: Why?
HENRY: My muscles.
THERAPIST: Would you like to be very strong?
HENRY: Twenty times as strong as all the people in the world put together!
THERAPIST: What else would you like to be?
HENRY: To have wings as hard as diamonds that could cut through anything.

When given "When I grow up I'd like to be..." as a lead-in, he said a policeman or a soldier or an astronaut. Policemen and soldiers in particular have to be "strict" and, as you'll see, "Me as I'd like to be" is extremely strict. Many children of Henry's age make little distinction between themselves now and as they'd like to be, perhaps having difficulty in imagining themselves different from what they are. As he rated "Me as I am now" in the middle for quite a few of his constructs, however, and was quite definitely at one extreme or the other for most with "Me as I'd like to be" there is quite a big difference. It is often said that rating at the mid-point means that the person doesn't really know where to place himself or another element. In Henry's case he was quite clear that

"3" meant sometimes he could be at one pole and sometimes another. He could be nice or nasty, funny or serious, kind or unkind, happy or sad, brave or a coward, depending on how the mood took him.

Marion's rating, as if she were Henry, shows quite a close understanding of how he saw people. Her rating of how he sees her is very similar, although she was surprised (and rather pleased) that he saw her as "not strict", as she felt that she was always having to chivvy him. *Her* rating of her husband is more favourable than his. He sees his father as unkind and weak, which gave her pause for thought. As Henry's construing of *"strong* vs *weak"* was basically physical, his rating his father "4" was probably due to the fact that he was disabled. In another part of the structured conversation the lead-in was: "The best thing about Daddy is ... H: That he has a car and he's disabled and we can go near everything, even without a meter!"

Marion realised that she herself was using the construct more psychologically and this led to her considering how Henry must often use words differently from herself.

Henry's self-characterisation was short and to the point:

> "My name is Henry. I live in London with my mother and my father and I wish they'd let us have a cat in the flat. My best friend is Denny and we are sometimes silly in class and get told off. I like fighting and want to be as strong as possible. It makes me sad that I can't talk properly and I want to talk like other people. I talk the normal way for quite a long time and then I start to chop up the words and people laugh."

It is unusual for a disfluent child of this age to place so much emphasis on speech and this, as well as his including the construct *"I talk well with* vs *I don't talk so well with"* in his grid, indicates that he was already construing his stuttering as an important factor in his view of himself.

Marion also wrote a long sketch of her son, in which she spoke of her fears for his future, how little attention he received from other adults besides herself, how his teachers thought he was not very bright because he didn't put his hand up in class. She was worried by the teasing which occurred at school which Henry reacted to by withdrawal or, if really provoked, by fighting. She wrote at some length about Henry's determination to be "strong"—initially fussy about food he would now eat anything so long as she assured him that it would "make him strong". She also spoke of his gentleness with younger children and babies and his love for his five-year-old cousin Tim (who is very strong, very nice and one of the few definitely happy people in his grid). She showed concern about Henry's earlier dislike of his father but saw him as getting on much better with him now, describing their wrestling together in the mornings. (When I did meet the father, some time later, they wrestled then and it seemed to me that there was a good deal of ambivalence on both sides in their "play".) Marion ended her sketch of Henry with comments about his speech. She was clearly puzzled by his disfluency and noted that he was at his best when talking to his toys or "when he lapses into baby talk".

By the end of the six exploratory sessions Henry said that he was happy to go on coming as it was much more fun than the last one. Marion felt that the interest taken in what Henry was like as a person was very important and she liked the fact that she could do much to help but at the same time shared the responsibility with someone else. It was now the summer holidays and they were going away, so we agreed to meet regularly from September up until Christmas and to work both on fluency and Henry's difficulties at school, mainly to do with relationships. Father had reluctantly agreed that we should continue, although still clinging to the belief that Henry would grow out of it anyway. I noticed that himself occasionally stuttered quite severely even now and he seemed very threatened by the experience, glowering at me as if daring me to comment. Of course I didn't.

The plan of action

A plan was drawn up largely on the basis of our sessions together, with the grid, the structured conversation, the self-characterisation and sketch and some drawings Henry had done providing useful material. He clearly needed to work directly on controlling his speech, but this would only be tolerable if "speaking smoothly" felt better than chopping the words up. He had missed out on the sort of attention any child needs so it seemed important that speaking smoothly should be validated at least by the adults in his life. The aunt in the grid was apparently fond of him but inclined to ignore him, talking away to his mother. She was slightly deaf and found Henry difficult to understand. So one aim was for him to speak so clearly to her that she would bother to listen. His father grew impatient when he stuttered so speaking smoothly to him would also be an advantage. Henry often wanted to say things in class but was afraid to in case he got stuck. He read well and fluently by now so the first step here was to offer to take his turn in class instead of being passed over. He stumbled badly the first time but wouldn't give up. Subsequently his reading went very well and his contribution to classroom conversation developed naturally from this first experiment.

The teasing was something else to be tackled as soon as possible as he could not yet hope to be fluent always when speaking to the other boys. We looked at all the different ways he could respond to teasing and acted them out in role-play. (When we considered the pros and cons of "the fighting approach" I had a taste of his "strength", playing the part of his disliked class-mate!) Withdrawal clearly wouldn't do any more—it was too close to "a coward, scared" to Henry's mind, but a dignified silence with a bored look proved acceptable. Joining in the laughter was tried and surprisingly seemed to work. Against his mother's better judgement he also became adept at finding something to tease his opponent about. Within a few weeks the teasing issue seemed to have become much less acute.

This gave us the opportunity to look at how Henry might develop easier relationships. He had only the haziest notion of what "friends" might be like and the most useful source for elaboration here was fiction. He loved adventure stories and I began to draw his attention to the relationships between the children in them as well as the exciting action. It has been found that children of his age don't use many "psychological" constructs when describing each other, but he was able to clarify how they behaved towards one another, the things they did together. They "rescued" each other from danger, they fought off the enemy together, shared what they had, especially secrets. He seemed to have no difficulty in translating these actions into possible school situations, so his new constructs really did have meaning in his own context.

It seemed that, up until now, Henry had been rather passive in relationships, waiting for others to come to him, even failing to respond to others' suggestions if he was unsure of the outcome. He gradually began to initiate more and learned to cope with "rejection" if his ideas were not always taken up. At one stage his teacher, although pleased to see him "coming out of his shell", expressed some concern to his mother about his "imaginative" suggestions for activities during free play periods. Mother explained something of what we were doing to her and she took care to validate his new assertion even if she had to play down one or two of his wilder schemes.

During one of the early sessions Henry had been asked to draw a picture of when he felt good and when he was the opposite. Figures 10.3 and 10.4 below reproduce these drawings.

In the first he is "at a party" and sitting with his friend (Denny?). There are streamers and balloons and lots of food on the table. In the second, the "bored" picture, he is alone except for three taller figures some way away. This seemed vividly to portray his discomfort when "left out" in adult company and paralleled something his mother had written in her sketch. Marion commented that Henry was invited to very few parties and then mentioned that he had never had a birthday party of his own, but was always taken out by his parents for "a treat" instead. Their flat was small and they couldn't afford to take a party of children out. Nevertheless, with his eighth birthday coming up, Marion was determined that he should have at least a few children home and that there would be streamers and balloons. There was a tussle with father, but he eventually agreed. As a result, Henry was invited back to other parties, as is the way of the world. Marion also took stock of the amount of time the boy spent as the odd one out in adult company and took steps to arrange for him to have a friend in on some of these occasions.

Figure 10.3 "When I feel good" drawing

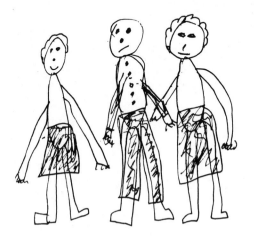

Figure 10.4 "I am bored" drawing

The outcome

Henry certainly benefited from his own and his mother's new approach to things and, by Christmas, seemed largely to have caught up socially and to be growing in confidence with his peers and with the teachers at school. Speaking smoothly was certainly proving worth the effort and he was able to slip into it more and more naturally. So, what more was there? When I asked Marion whether we should cut down the sessions after Christmas and gradually phase out she seemed reluctant. There was one more area she wanted to "sort out". And that was the relationship between the three of them. *Was* she in fact over-protective of Henry, particularly in relation to her husband? Could I help her stand up to him better on her own behalf? This was a very different issue, so we agreed that Marion should come alone for some sessions and that Henry should come every three weeks to extend the work he was doing and make sure that all was going well.

The sessions with Marion don't belong to this account but they resulted in considerable experiment on her part in handling things differently with her husband. They seem to have talked together for the first time at any length about his bitterness at his disablement—she had always avoided mentioning it where she could, thinking this was best. And she hadn't realised what it meant to this "strong" man to be unable to do the things he had done in his youth. She understood that his pressure on Henry was some kind of compensation for his own loss and was able to negotiate some changes with him. I only saw the father once more myself and his manner was as scornful as ever towards "this therapy nonsense". But he *had* changed towards Henry, largely, I'm sure, through being able to communicate some of his feelings to his wife.

By April, Henry was coming once a month and we had our last session together in July before the summer holidays. He was now eight years old and had decided that though seven-year-olds might chop their words up eight-year-olds didn't do so. As a final note, Marion said that, after his birthday, Henry no longer used baby-talk—a ploy which had enabled him to be fluent earlier. We kept in touch for some time and a letter from

Marion several years later told of Henry's thriving and enjoying life at a new school, where he had just begun to do drama.

The time-scale of a year and three months, with sessions gradually spaced out, is a fair example of therapy which combines speech modification work with counselling for a child of this age, already construing his stammer as a problem. Things don't always turn out so well, of course, for a number of reasons. Here we had a mother who contributed a great deal and was willing herself to change. (Peggy Dalton (22) shows further examples of therapy where the mother's part is seen as crucial to the process.) Henry had some clear superordinate constructs about how things should be for him which could be used as guidelines when planning experiments. He also proved himself well able to create new constructs, such as those to do with friends. Despite the father's opposition, changes in the mother led to changes in their relationship which were helpful all round. There are many examples in Tom Ravenette's writings (e.g. Reference (40)) of his sessions with children and young people which show different problems with varying solutions. He may sometimes see a child only once, get him or her to draw around the situation, talk about it and send the child off with something to think about. Although he will always follow up with the school to check on how the child is doing, they may not actually meet again. In others of his studies, counselling may be focused on a story which Tom Ravenette tells in response to what the child brings. This imaginative approach, again, leaves the child with a new light on his or her predicament. In still other cases, of course, resolution of the problem at school takes longer and a wide range of exploratory and reconstruction processes are used, but the aim is basically to help all concerned to understand each other better and thereby change their approach to one another.

Sarah

The story

Sarah was an attractive, lively woman in her early thirties. On her first visit, she inspected the furnishings, gave advice on the cat and questioned me keenly on my qualifications and experience. In most respects, she was enjoying a full and successful life. She worked in film production and was pleased with the way things were going. She had good friends and good relationships with her parents and younger sister. She had recently bought a new flat and was "having a wonderful time" decorating it and making it just as she wanted it. Even as she painted this glowing picture she commented that perhaps she oughtn't to be coming to see me at all—she was very lucky. "The problem" was a long time ago.

At the age of ten Sarah had been sexually abused by a neighbour. He was a middle-aged man who lived alone after the death of his wife and whom her family scarcely knew. She told no-one of the incident and soon afterwards he was in trouble because of another child and they saw no more of him. Her mother asked her if he had ever approached her or her sister and Sarah said no. She had a feeling to this day that her mother wasn't satisfied, but it was never mentioned again.

Later, in her teens, Sarah took a dislike to boys and had only female friends. She dismissed boys as "stupid" and "oafish" and when she went to university she made no male friends there for the first two years. Then, during her third year, she started to go out with a young man and for a short time was very happy in his company. When she began to feel that he was attracted to her (and she to him?) she became afraid and when he attempted to kiss her one night she was sick. She avoided close contact with men after this for about two years, although she had quite good working relationships with men at in her job. Then she began another relationship and the same pattern of fear and sickness recurred. She thought at this time of finding some help and of talking to her mother about it, but decided against both. She read everything she could on the subject and hoped that "next time" she would be able to cope.

Then she met a man at work whom she immediately felt drawn to and was convinced that everything would be all right with him. It was—and they enjoyed a rewarding sexual relationship for about a year and became engaged. Then, without warning, he left her for someone else and moved away from London.

She never really understood what happened and made light of it to her friends. At first Sarah didn't feel too much. She was "sad" and missed him, but the experience had been a good one and she had proved to herself that she was "normal" and could push the past away.

A few months later, a man made a pass at her during a party and she fainted. It had all started again. After this she thought more and more about the man who had gone away and became very depressed. She spoke to no-one at first and believes that no-one realised how she was feeling. Then a friend was telling her about her own therapy and she made up her mind, at last, to seek help. She wanted to "blot out the past once and for all".

When she had told her story, I outlined the personal construct approach and she agreed to four exploratory sessions so that we could gain a better idea of what might be involved, how long we might need to work together and so on. I also asked her to try to remember how she was as a child of ten, in an attempt to see what she might have brought to the experience at the time. She had feared that I would get her to describe the incident in detail and was relieved that I hadn't. I suggested that it would probably be a matter of trying to make more sense of the effect of what had happened on her, not to push it away, but to leave it behind as something which was over and need not continue to interfere with relationships. I also asked her to write a self-characterisation.

Exploring the problem

Sarah's self-characterisation begins with a physical description of herself:

> "Sarah is 5'2" tall, green eyes, red hair, slim build and with nothing distinctive about her."

She goes on to speak of her family in affectionate terms. She expresses concern about her father's illness but admiration for his courage and humour. She records the death of her grandfather as the first major loss of her life three years before and how unlike herself she was in feeling it so deeply and for so long. She had been very close to him. She then describes the relationship with her fiancé and while the sadness is there at his leaving her, she expresses no anger. She ends:

> "Sarah has a fairly wide circle of friends of whom she is very fond and to whom she looks for different things. They see her as rather eccentric, living alone, but she would say that this was her independence and self-reliance. She is happy in her own company and would rather read or amuse herself than go out with others just for the sake of it."

She could not remember a great deal about herself at 10 years, but thought she was quite bright and "sporty" and something of a tom-boy compared with her sister. She remembered feeling "very low" about herself after the assault and, for a while, she had done very badly at school. She had always got on well with her parents and thought that perhaps one of the worst things about the incident was her lying to her mother. She wanted, even now, to pluck up courage to tell both her parents. She was sure that they would be sympathetic and not "disgusted" with her but she had always been too afraid. She once almost told her sister but had held back at the last minute. The only person she *had* told was her fiancé and he had seemed to understand her and the effect it had had on her. In that second session she also said a good deal about her work and it was clear that she was extremely competent and highly regarded.

We began to elicit constructs for a grid which she rated at home during the third and fourth sessions and posted to me so that I could analyse it for the last of our agreed exploratory meetings.

When we went through the grid, Sarah was pleased to see that the elements "Me now" and "Me without my problem" were "on the same side". There were only three major differences in her rating of the two. Using a nine-point scale, you will see that she placed "Me now" at the mid-point and "Me without my problem" on 1 for the construct *"honest* vs *deceitful"*. For *"easy to understand* vs *hard to understand"* "Me now" is again at

'Sarah'

1 ——————— 5   5 ——————— 9

(1 pole)	Mother	Sally	Father	Di	Cedric	Me now	Grandfather	Delia	Derek	Pat	Tim	Brenda	John	Steve	June	Me without my problem	Janice	Kate	Alison	(9 pole)
can be myself with	8	1	7	1	2	1	3	1	7	1	2	8	1	6	1	1	3	2	3	have to hold back
extrovert	9	2	6	3	6	5	6	5	7	4	3	7	6	4	7	5	5	2	1	quiet
knows what he/she wants	2	2	5	3	4	3	5	2	1	4	8	9	7	1	1	3	5	2	1	drifting
honest	1	2	1	2	2	5	1	1	7	2	5	6	1	8	2	1	2	2	7	deceitful
aware of self-image	2	2	5	3	5	4	5	6	1	2	7	8	2	2	2	2	3	2	1	mercurial
easy to understand	1	2	1	2	2	5	4	3	6	3	1	2	1	7	2	2	4	3	1	hard to understand
tough	5	1	6	1	6	5	2	1	4	1	7	9	5	1	5	3	4	2	1	flabby
sharp	5	1	2	1	2	2	3	1	6	1	7	8	2	7	3	2	5	3	7	dull
falls apart publicly	4	2	9	8	9	9	8	7	2	8	2	2	9	3	8	7	6	6	4	private
challenging	3	1	2	1	3	1	1	1	6	1	5	8	1	7	3	1	5	2	6	not stimulating
sure of self	5	2	5	2	3	2	2	3	8	3	7	9	1	3	5	2	3	2	7	easily swayed
undemonstrative	1	7	1	7	4	3	2	2	5	4	8	2	7	6	7	8	9	7	9	physically demonstrative
eccentric	7	6	5	8	9	7	7	8	9	5	4	9	8	6	5	5	6	9	3	ordinary
self-reliant	2	8	6	6	8	2	1	5	9	2	7	9	5	8	5	4	6	6	8	needs someone 'there'
soft, gentle	3	3	4	3	2	4	1	3	6	4	2	2	2	4	3	2	1	3	6	brash
inspires trust	3	2	5	2	2	2	1	2	6	2	1	7	1	7	2	2	1	3	6	frothy
makes time for people	2	4	5	3	5	3	2	4	6	2	3	6	4	7	3	2	1	3	8	selfish
aware	5	2	3	2	3	1	1	2	8	1	4	8	1	2	3	1	2	2	5	insensitive

Figure 10.5 Sarah's grid

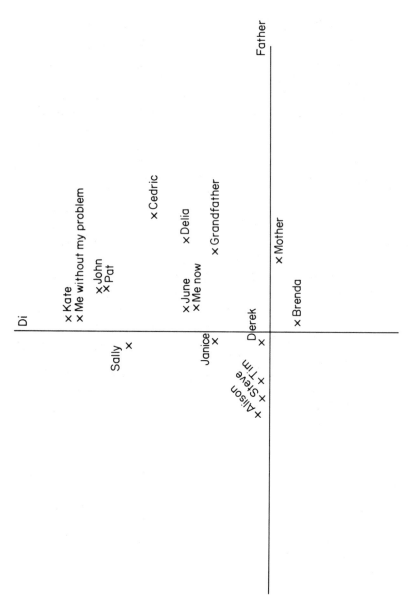

Figure 10.6 Relationship between the elements in Sarah's grid

the mid-point and "Me without my problem" is rated 2. For "*undemonstrative* vs *physically demonstrative*" "Me now" is seen as 3 (fairly undemonstrative) and "Me without my problem" as 8 (very physically demonstrative). It struck her that if she were honest she would automatically be easier to understand and she would feel free to be physically demonstrative. When she thought about not being able to call herself honest now, she could only say that it was because people didn't know about her childhood. People? No—her mother. People as a whole did not need to know. This made her even more determined to talk to her mother. (This is an example of a process of reducing the permeability of a powerful construct and, thus, reducing its damaging implications.)

The relationships between all the other elements made sense to her and Sarah felt that the "toughness" implied by many of her constructs represented the kind of person others saw her to be, especially the men with whom she worked. In fact, she confessed that she tended to blame herself if anything went wrong at work, although she felt competent in what she did. She said how unassertive she was in the face of anger. She and some of her women friends knew that she was on the gentle side, rather than "brash" but she thought she would be more gentle if she were free of her problem. The toughness was something of a protection. Being "private" as opposed to "falling apart publicly" was very important to her and quite different, she thought, from being deceitful. She had found the whole process of doing the grid fascinating and, as so often happens, there were no real surprises in the outcome, only confirmation of the way she saw things. But where would we go from here?

The major problem, seemed to be one of guilt in the face both of the traumatic experience itself and lying to her mother. The anxiety which led to her reactions to encounters with men seemed to spring as much from not knowing how to handle a "normal" situation as from her memories of that event. Doubts about her sexuality were strong. Although having healthy self-respect in some areas, her lack of assertion in the face of others' anger and the tendency to bury her own strong feelings suggested an unsureness about being able to deal with emotions linked with these doubts.

We looked at what connection she could see between how she had felt after the assault and how she felt once the loss of her fiancé had dawned on her, since these were two key periods when she seemed to have lost confidence in herself and become depressed. She responded immediately with "Why me?" She remembered wondering why, as a child, the neighbour had chosen her, what had she done? And she had asked herself the same question when the man she was going to marry had left her. She had never felt angry with John and, realised for the first time, never felt angry with the her neighbour. Only frightened and very confused. How much of this doubt was left? There were a few things which linked here. First, her reactions to trouble at work. Then, although attractive and with an eye for colour, she wore clothes which more or less swamped her. She felt people would be less inclined to look at her ("with nothing distinctive about her"?) She had never been very good at dealing with compliments from men. She had learned not to back away and adopted a jokey, sarcastic response instead, but was not comfortable.

So these two aspects—her embarrassment and her lack of assertion in some situations seemed important starting points. We agreed that we should begin in these areas which seemed manageable, rather than plunge into the heart of her fear of sexual contact.

The experiments

Over the next few weeks, during which we were able to meet three times owing to her travelling with her job, Sarah set about reconstruing how she dressed and dealing with the resultant comments. To her relief, she found that men didn't immediately pounce on her and she decided that she was probably no more "sexual" in more feminine clothes than in her former "sacks". She tried various ways of responding to compliments, but one of the most helpful things was when she began, quite spontaneously, to compliment others, men and women, not only on how they looked but on the things they did. This had the effect of taking the "false spotlight" off herself. She also tried to deal with the odd explosion which occurred on set more effectively and, although still rather frightened if someone became angry, was standing her ground better. She announced in triumph at the beginning of one session that she had "lost her temper" with a cameraman and felt great when he apologised to her.

Then came a two-month break while she was abroad. She had visited her parents on her return before coming to the session and had spoken to her mother about the assault. As she had known, her mother had no feelings of "disgust" and only felt sorry that Sarah hadn't been able to talk to her at the time. She told her what she knew of the neighbour, whom she had seen as unbalanced owing to his wife's death. This seemed to help Sarah believe that she had not been to blame. She left her mother to tell her father in her own time. This had obviously been very important and Sarah wanted to rerate the grid and change herself now to "1" for honest.

We met twice more before Sarah was to take up a new job in the North. She did not feel she needed to be referred on as she was much more comfortable with herself now in many ways. She had not yet started a close relationship but had been out with one or two men while she was away. One incident had brought together the work she was doing on both her sexuality and her assertion. A man had suggested they sleep together after one evening out and she refused. When he asked her if she was "frigid", she was able to face up to him, tell him that he didn't appeal to her and retire gracefully, "shaking like hell" but not in a panic. She felt really angry at the insult and had been able, she thought, to deal with it as her "adult self" rather than her ten-year-old child. She predicted that, in time, she would meet someone again with whom she could relate well. The last I heard was a year later when, on a cryptic post-card, she wrote that "the old devil is finally in his box with the lid soldered on!"

Summary

As we have said, most of the work in this and other kinds of therapy goes on outside the sessions. We only met a dozen times in all over a period of five months and Sarah made some substantial changes in that time and clearly went on changing after it. Our work together was related to clarification, planning and reflecting on the outcomes of events in her experiments. It was clear from our exploratory sessions that, although the event which brought her had had a devastating effect on her, there were many strengths and resources for her to call upon. She had a number of roles in which she felt confident and at ease—her work role (apart from her difficulty with anger), her friendships, her role as a daughter. Her "problem", although relating to a very core part of her, was *not* invading every aspect of her life. This, and her willingness to work, made reconstruction possible. Once again, the basis of that reconstruction rested on awareness of the importance of particular issues for her.

Fran

The history

Fran telephoned for an appointment because she had a "weight problem" and wanted to do something about it. When she came, however, it soon emerged that this was the least of her problems. She had only just managed to drive herself to the appointment, being often totally unable to leave the house. She was extremely depressed, had had "a major collapse" a few months before, which resulted in some months in hospital. She was acutely anxious about many "trivial" things and, above all, hated to be alone. All this had been going on for about twenty years (she was in her late forties) and she basically had very little hope that anything could change for her.

Amongst this anguished torrent (she talked incessantly), there was very little about herself which she valued. She was, apparently, "brilliant" at Cambridge, but thoroughly unhappy. Before she married she had had some success with graphic art, but given it all up as soon as she could. After the birth of her first child "the real depression" began, although she spoke highly of both her children and of her husband "who couldn't be kinder, but doesn't know what to do with me". It also emerged, quite casually, that Fran had, for a while, been involved with the care of young drug users and found a good deal of satisfaction in the work. But she gave that up too, against everyone else's wishes, when she decided that she was too "hopeless" herself to be of any use to others. This was clearly going to be very complex and, if she wanted to work on herself, a very long process. But we agreed first on six exploratory sessions, after which we would try to see what could be done and what she wanted to "leave alone" as she put it. During this period Fran wrote prolifically and very movingly of her feelings and of the many events in her life which she regretted and felt guilty about. It was quite difficult to get her to focus on preparing a grid, but it seemed a useful structure through which we might be able to draw something together to work on. Figure 10.7 shows clearly her position in her own eyes in relation to all the people of whom she thought well.

The two selves she chose to include were "Me as I usually am" and "Me as I can be", but they were both rated negatively on many constructs. The system was tight, with a large first component of constructs which correlated highly with one another and, as you see, with a large group of elements seen as similar to one another. It seemed very likely that there was some real threat to her in being "confident", "contented with herself" or "liking the world" so we used Finn Tschudi's ABC technique for exploring implicative dilemmas. The following examples probably speak for themselves:

A: confident needing approval, confirmation

B: (advantages) (disadvantages)
—independent —dependent
—can be alone —unsure of yourself
—not afraid of things —not able to cope

C: (disadvantages) (advantages)
—people won't help —it means you are humble
—people make demands —people like you to turn
  on you   to them
—too much is expected —they don't think you are
     big-headed

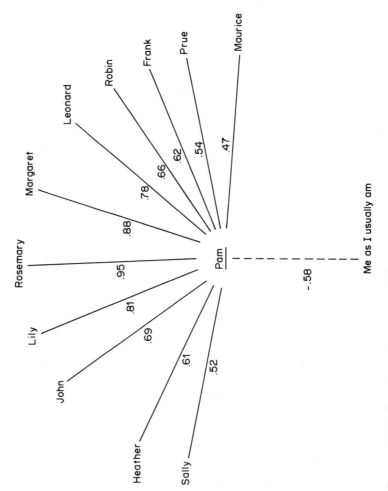

Figure 10.7   Fran's main group of elements

A: free, contented with self   depressed

B: (advantages)   (disadvantages)
—not such a pain to others   —people are tired of you
—self-reliant, happy   —you can't enjoy anything

C: (disadvantages)   (advantages)
—you have to be hard   —when I'm depressed I don't
—likely to be insensitive   try new things and
—you haven't suffered   face failure
—I suppose my husband does
still love me when I'm
unhappy

When we came to explore *"liking the world* vs *afraid of going out and meeting people"*, on being asked for the advantages of "liking the world", Fran burst into tears and said: "how can I, it's so ghastly!".

This came out during the fifth session and Fran said "How can you change all that?". Nevertheless, during the sixth session she said that she did want to go on, it did help to talk and perhaps we could just make *something* better. I asked her what she thought she could change and what, for the moment, she saw as having to remain the same. After some thought she said that she could perhaps do more, could at least find an area of happiness and be less of a drag on her husband.

What could be done?

The picture was one of extreme constriction and the limitation of Fran's experience during many years made sense of her anxiety—she simply did not know how to cope with the unknown. The guilt she expressed in her writing suggested dislodgement of very long standing. She could not express an ideal self but there must have been one for her to feel that she had fallen so far short of what she *ought* to have been. Her dependency was crippling. Although she relied mainly on her husband these days it was clear that, when she had friends, she had also leaned heavily on them. Although when her children were growing up she felt that she had been a "supportive" mother, she did not see herself as having a role for them now.

Nevertheless, having made up her mind to aim for limited change, Fran proved surprisingly willing to get down to work. She talked less incessantly and thought a great deal more. She said more than once that she feared "enormous change", she knew herself as she was and she wanted to go very slowly. As we looked at what she could do to enhance her life without threatening her too much it appeared that she had always loved drawing and painting but had let it all go when she married. She began to draw again and although she almost gave it up several times as she was "so bad", she did continue and seemed to have found that "area of happiness" she was looking for. While she was absorbed in it she found she did not mind if she was alone. Later, she joined a local art group but only after a good deal of work on how she was going to cope with getting there and relating to the other people. She said that she would like to go "as someone else", which seemed to ask for something along the lines of an approach which Kelly developed but which has been relatively little used.

Fixed role therapy

Kelly's fixed role therapy has been referred to in Chapter 7. As we saw, it is a technique based on the person's original self-description where a new "character" is created for the client to develop and play, just as an experiment. The character should not be an idealisation of the self or someone totally divorced from the client's experience. It should, rather, be someone whom the client would like to know, would have some understanding of and whose life-style it would be possible to adopt. As Kelly envisaged the process, the person was to develop the character during therapy sessions through role-play and "live" it for two weeks, with frequent meetings with the therapist during that time. The aim was to experience change, not an attempt to alter the personality for ever. After the two weeks the client goes back to normal.

There was no question of our embarking on the full experiment, but it did seem a way to help Fran approach a new experience. Based on her self-characterisation, which was full of self-recrimination and despair, but with one or two important positive self-references, such as to her "kindness", "sensitivity" and "supportiveness", the following sketch called "Jessica" was drawn up with her approval:

"Jessica is a warm person, quiet and a little shy, but you always know that she is listening to you and interested in you. She enjoys creative things and especially loves to draw and see other people's drawing and painting. She likes to do it well, but can take it if she makes mistakes or doesn't like what she has done. She will go on until she gets it right and encourage others to do the same.

Although she has had many problems and is not always very happy now, she is able to put this unhappiness aside when she is with others and seldom speaks of her difficulties, unless she is sure that the other person would understand and would really want to know. She knows how to live in the present and take life as it comes."

This short sketch is not perhaps a typical fixed role sketch, as it was written for a more limited and particular purpose. It was meant only as a means of helping Fran to approach the art class with less fear. But some of the points emphasised would hopefully have some effect on other aspects of her life. For example, it seemed important for her to listen to others and respond to their needs more, rather than launch into her own tale of sorrow, as she tended to. There was a danger of her being too quickly disheartened by any "failure", so aiming to be the sort of person who wants to get things right but doesn't take it badly when all isn't perfect, also seemed important in this situation. Living in the present was the most crucial part of all, as the aim was for Fran to enjoy the classes for their own sake and not take her whole history in with her.

She enjoyed the experience and even made an effort to "dress the part" in casual but attractive clothes. She found it helped her to call herself Jessica when asked her name and no-one ever knew that she was Fran. Instead of being limited to two weeks, Fran was able to develop this "character" over time and found that she could stick to it while she was at the classes and even carry over some of the aspects into other situations in her life.

In particular, she listened better to others, which had the effect of taking the emphasis off her own shortcomings. She made one or two new friends for the first time for years. It did not transform her life, but it helped. She still became very depressed at times, but even then could look forward to the depression's lifting—something she had been unable to do before.

How far could we go?

Fran came for therapy over a period of two years, with a few breaks for holidays. At no stage did she change her mind about any radical attempt at reconstruction and all along resisted exploring early relationships and difficulties in an attempt to make more sense of how she came to be as she was. Although regretting her dependence on others, particularly her husband, she felt that it would be too threatening to try to alter this. She only hoped that he would outlive her! And yet her life *was* better in a number of ways. She was doing more, as she wanted all those sessions ago, she had found some happiness and she was at least able to reconstrue being "a drag" on her husband. Their relationship, she perceived, suited them both. Her art thrived and later she began teaching others.

SO HOW *DOES* IT ALL END?

Not always happily ever after of course. These are just three very different examples of a PCP approach to therapy and others in the literature illustrate the wide variety of aims and outcomes (see below). As can be seen from these, the aims are different because the clients and their needs are different. The outcomes vary because what they were able to give to the process varied. One of the things our three studies have in common is the focus on their own construing systems and another is the way in which all the clients brought their share of creativity and experiment to what we did. The process did not end at our last meetings, even in Fran's case. They all took away at least some of the experience of change and a knowledge of what experiment could mean. Henry and Sarah clearly went on doing their own thing. Fran held on to what she had gained and was able to some extent to build on it.

If you find single case studies helpful to your understanding of the processes of change in this type of therapy, here are references to some others:

'Luke' in *Personal Change and Reconstruction* by Fay Fransella (Academic Press, 1972) Here, she describes her work with an adult who stuttered.

'The case of Sue' in *Personal Construct Psychology: Psychotherapy and Personality* edited by Landfield and Leitner (Wiley, 1980) In this example, Leitner shows personal construct treatment of a severely disturbed woman.

'Mike' also by Larry Leitner in *Personal Construct Therapy Casebook*, edited by Neimeyer and Neimeyer (Springer, 1987).

'Clare' by Maureen Sheehan, in *Repertory Grid Technique and Personal Constructs*, edited by Nigel Beail (Croom Helm, 1985). This is an account of the process of change in the self-construing of a depressed patient.

In Tom Ravenette's papers referred to earlier there are many vignettes of work with individual children and young people.

CAN IT BE USED
IN GROUPS?

With the emphasis on the personal construing of each individual, it might seem that PCP would be an unsuitable approach for groups of people to use. But those of you who have come with us so far will probably realise that other emphases within Kelly's psychology are of equal importance: the need we all have to understand each other's views if we are to get on together (sociality), the inevitable overlap between the construing of one person and another in many situations (commonality); and the whole area of the effects of interaction with others on the development of any one person's construing of themselves and their worlds. All these and many other facets of this approach make it eminently relevant for work in groups.

KELLY'S APPROACH TO GROUP THERAPY

Kelly himself (1) sees the main function of group psychotherapy as broadly the same as those of any form of therapy or counselling:

> "to assist the person to develop more effective channels through which he and others may anticipate events."

He goes on to point out:

> "Since such a large portion of the events to be anticipated are human events, group psychotherapy, like most psychotherapy, deals particularly with the improvement of one's anticipations of his fellow man. This is not

only because our fellow men are such busy inventive people—always making unexpected things happen—but also because each of us has dispersed his dependencies so widely among his neighbours. Keeping up with the world has become a very complicated business, altogether too much for a person who relies on antiquated ideas."

He also suggests some strong advantages in working with groups in this way. As a *base for experimentation* the group, with its contrasting personalities, affords each client more scope for development of a new, more comprehensive role. It gives all members the opportunity for *discrimination*. They can discover which of their constructs can be applied to several persons (i.e., are permeable) and which are applicable only to a few (impermeable). *Pre-emptive* construing, where a person makes a snap judgement, say, about a certain person or type of person, is also challenged in the group situation more easily, perhaps, than when there are only two people working together. Similarly, *constellatory* construing, which we have likened to stereotyping, can be thrown into question where there are people present who do not fit into some pattern that a member has formed for them. For example, someone who has always considered fat people to be "happy-go-lucky, self-satisfied, materialistic and lazy", may have to think again about that large man or woman in the group who shows every sign of being quite different from the stereotype.

We have spoken (Chapter 7) of the importance of a variety of *validational* evidence, both positive and negative, for anyone who wants to experiment with something new. In a group, a client learns to value both in order to clarify his or her views. At first, we may only look for confirmation of how we have always seen ourselves and others but, with a group that is working well together, disconfirmation becomes acceptable and useful. This implies another very important development—that of the ability to disperse our dependencies. This may be the most crucial first step for some clients who especially need to learn to discriminate between their dependencies and to distribute them appropriately among a number of people. Some experience most of their trouble in life because they put all their eggs in one basket (as in obsessive sexual relationships), others have difficulty because they continually dump all their eggs in so many baskets at once that they are totally confused as to what "advice" to follow. Still others find it hard to depend on anyone but themselves and have no-one to turn to when they are confused and unhappy.

Kelly also outlines six phases in the development of group psychotherapy:

1. Initiation of mutual support
2. Initiation of primary role relationships (the development of sociality amongst members)
3. Initiation of mutual primary enterprises (experiments within the group sessions)
4. Exploration of personal problems
5. Exploration of secondary roles (role relationships outside the group)
6. Exploration of secondary enterprises (experiments outside the group)

He points out that although, as the group goes on, one can often see these phases clearly developing in sequence, they do overlap and there are some sessions which seem to exhibit all six phases at once. We have found, each of us working with a different type of group, that these "phases" are perhaps the least useful of Kelly's ideas for groups. The processes he describes within these phases, such as the development of support between members and the initiating of joint experiments undoubtedly occur, but we have not found it helpful to plan such a sequence, even in outline. In our experience, the exploration of personal problems for some members, for example, always begins very early on. But his suggestions on a group's functions and advantages have certainly added new dimensions to our therapy with groups and contributed much to other experiments with groups where the aim has been to solve some organisational problem, for instance, rather than being "therapeutic" in the strictest sense.

Kelly discusses in detail such issues as the development of mutual *acceptance* amongst members, the use of enactment for initiating primary role relationships, dealing with the threat and possible hostility that will arise and so on. He also looks at problems which are special to group therapy such as the integration of a client who comes into the group some time after it has started; problems involved with combining discussion with enactment or role-play, where the two need to be kept clearly distinct. One thing which emerges with great clarity, as with all Kelly's proposals for therapeutic procedures, is the need for *planning* of experiments, evaluation of outcomes and creative modification in the light of the outcomes. And again, these are the concerns of the whole group, not just the therapist. Here too it is a *joint* enterprise.

Experiments in PCP Group Therapy

There are by now many examples in the literature of group work run along PCP lines, few of them staying closely within Kelly's original framework of phases described above, most developing his ideas in a number of directions but still guided by the most important principles of therapeutic interaction. Some groups have been for people with a variety of psychological problems, some for more homogeneous groups, with eating disorders, alcoholism, stuttering, for example, in common. We shall describe some of these experiments briefly and see what they have in common, how they differ and to what extent we may say that Kelly's ideas have been the major influence on their progress.

A PCP Group in Action

Gavin Dunnett with Sue Llewelyn (41), after considering the advantages of this approach in theory, set up a group for seven clients having a range of problems, with the intention of using Kelly's framework as a whole and his guidelines for groups in particular. They present details of their own anticipations, the clients involved and the sixteen sessions undertaken. For those who are interested in following the ups and downs of a therapy group at work, this is perhaps the fullest account in the PCP literature. Activities planned to facilitate understanding and experiment, including dyadic interactions followed by role-play to the whole group of what each partner had "heard" from the other are described. Possibly the most unusual aspect of this presentation, however, is the degree to which the therapists show how the experience was for them personally. They conclude that while the venture was worthwhile it left a number of questions to be answered. In their view, it seemed to provide an individual methodology within a group setting, rather than a group methodology itself. It was helpful to understanding and working with the individual problems of the members and the group setting provided a useful social context in which reconstruing and experiment could take place. But except in relation to the first few sessions, the phases described by Kelly did not appear to have too much meaning. They suggest that "further elaboration and/or experiment is called for".

A PCP Group for People who Stutter

Peggy Dalton (42) made no attempt to structure a group for adults with fluency problems in line with Kelly's phases but used both PCP exploratory techniques and ideas for reconstruction in an attempt to address the extremely difficult problem of maintaining fluency once it has been established by behavioural means. It is notoriously easy for someone who stutters to achieve fluency while "on a programme", very much harder to transfer that fluency to everyday life and depressingly difficult for them to maintain fluency over time. It had seemed clear for some time that more than a change in behaviour is involved. A quite radical change in the construing of fluency, of communication in general, and, in some cases, of many aspects of the self must also be undertaken.

Through the use of grids and self-characterisations, individual members explored their own constructions, which they were invited to share with the others as and when they wished. Each clarified their own methods for modifying speech and one of the agreements was that no-one should attempt to influence the others in this, only encourage and, perhaps, remind them to use what they had chosen. Aims for the group sessions were drawn up together and, on the whole, followed faithfully. At first the focus was on their difficulties in various situations and in relation to various people in terms of speaking. Using role-play, currently ineffective ways of dealing with them were illustrated and alternative, more effective ways were tried out and refined. In between the sessions most of the members carried out these experiments in their daily lives.

Quite quickly the group became willing to share important constructions of things and, with one exception, far greater sociality was developed between them. They soon ceased to try to impose their views on one another and came to accept their differences as well as what they had in common. Laddering one another (see Chapter 7) was found to be very useful in this process and the ABC model threw up a number of dilemmas for several of them. Trying on new opposites for size or even taking on someone else's construct, just for the experience of looking at something afresh, also proved helpful. Although fixed role therapy as such was not embarked on, aspects of this approach, confined to specific situations, were used.

As the group progressed, our aims dilated. From a narrow focus on maintaining fluent speech, wider issues of communication and relationship were discussed and changes devised and tried out. It soon seemed clear that one of the problems with their earlier therapies, helpful though they had been as far as they went, was that very focus on speech and speech alone which kept them all preoccupied with themselves as speakers, rather than themselves as whole people with many other priorities and aspirations. Although this was only a small group, the first of its kind, and was not set up as a "controlled experiment" to prove the benefits of using a PCP approach, the results were promising and further work along these and more developed lines is being undertaken in the area of stuttering (43).

A Group for Women with Eating Disorders

Eric Button (21) has done a great deal of work with people, mainly women, who are anorexic or bulimic or who eat compulsively. He bases his personal construct approach to these disorders on three points of understanding:

(1) It may be useful to approach the person who presents with an "eating disorder" as someone who is aiming for some degree of predictability in her life.
(2) It is argued that both the concern with eating and the desire to control eating may become the main area in life where a person's predictions may be validated. The likelihood, however, is that where this arises there is a corresponding relative failure to predict people: this includes both the self and others.
(3) Therapeutic endeavours should primarily recognise the person's need to maintain some predictability through eating or eating control strategies. The extent to which the client will choose to explore the personal (and, by implication, interpersonal) side of her life will depend on the extent to which the client feels safe with the therapists. (Which in this group experiment also implied feeling safe with the group as a whole.)

He set up a group of eight women for a period of twenty weeks. Their ages ranged from 19 to 30, three were overweight, three underweight and two were of average weight. The aim of the group was to "elaborate personal construing" and was put to them as follows:

"Although all members of the group have difficulty associated with weight and eating, we will not be emphasising weight change and we will be aiming more at helping you to learn ways of being yourself and attaining your goals other than through eating and weight control."

(Which was very much how the group for people who stuttered developed.)

Eric Button used the model of the Interpersonal Transaction Group developed by Al Landfield and Clayton Rivers (44) where most of the work is done in "rotating dyads". This involves brief interactions in pairs where people are asked to talk to each other on some topic, such as, "What I like and dislike in people"; "Situations where I feel at ease and ill at ease". The aim of the dyads is for people to develop their understanding of each other in the hope that this understanding might generalise outside the group. One stipulation is that the members try to listen and understand and do not judge one another. The paired conversations in the Landfield and Rivers groups are interspersed with group discussion. Eric Button found that, as time went on, people wanted more time for group discussion, so dyads were discontinued.

Although it seems that most people realised the limitations of being preoccupied with eating, Eric Button felt that the relatively short duration of the group was probably not enough to bring about movement or to establish a full enough elaboration of person construing. The invalidation of the old constructs caused some confusion and anxiety in them all. He concluded that while such a group approach might be one way of "freeing the person from the cage that they had created with weight", therapeutic movement will be likely to require longer term help and in some cases considerable support "as they enter the world of people and relationships". It does seem, however, that this approach along PCT lines is worth pursuing in this very difficult area.

Groups for Those with Alcohol Dependence

Al Landfield and Clayton Rivers have described their group work with people with alcohol problems. They look at the difficulty in relation to the social context in which it usually develops. One effect of alcohol for most people is to lower anxiety: "the disinhibiting effect of the drug allows a sense of social freedom and comfort for the person utilising it". In PCP terms this may be seen as involving two processes:

> "a dilating and loosening of the construct system. These processes ... can be associated with greater flexibility, spontaneity, creativeness and sometimes, grandiosity, impulsiveness, and confusion."

A person who is socially inhibited may be constricted and tight in his or her construing and have real difficulty in both expressing himself or herself and construing others.

With these and other ideas in mind, these authors developed the Interpersonal Transaction method described above. As well as the dyadic interactions and group discussions, they use "mood tags" which the members pin onto themselves at the beginnings of sessions to indicate in what state of mind they have come to the group. Another procedure used during the first session was for members to introduce themselves to each other, communicating by gesture only, to emphasise that interaction consists of more than just words. They follow this with a discussion of the gesture session to see what it means to them. The overall aim of these sessions is, again, to develop greater understanding of the self and others and, additionally, to accept as positive the role of sobriety and to relegate alcohol use to a less important and even negative position in the members' lives. There is specific focus on change itself as a process since, as with those with eating disorders, simply challenging your current constructions is not enough and so radical a change can be frightening and painful.

One point which comes out strongly from one or two of the homogeneous groups described is the need for the emphasis to be taken off the problem shared by the members, once the reassurance and support gained through sharing has been established. In most other groups for eating disorders, for example, the focus seems to be centrally on eating and weight and what can be done about them. In Eric Button's group, as we saw, from the very beginning it was made clear that the emphasis would be on the difficulties of personal construing which had resulted from the preoccupation with food and weight. In the group for people who stuttered, the focus widened naturally.

The Range of PCP Group Therapy

Particularly in more recent years the use of a PCP approach to therapy with groups has widened. Pamela Alexander and

Victor Follette (45) for example gave an account of their work with women who have been the victims of incest as children. Although stressing, as others do, the importance in such homogeneous groups of the supportive nature of their shared problem, they are concerned that the reassurance that "one is not so different from other people" does not lead to even more focus on that one area of the members' self-construing. Especially in the case of incest, where many people may already be defining every aspect of their existence in terms of the incest experience, such extra emphasis may serve to justify and strengthen an ongoing cycle of victimisation. Part of their work on developing sociality, common to all groups, is therefore the clarification and discussion of the many differences in the constructions of the members. While the group processes described for this group are not startlingly different from those experienced in a non-PCP group, the therapists' use of grids among other assessment procedures for their understanding of individual members' views of themselves and their worlds does seem to have facilitated these aims for both sharing and distinguishing the self from others.

Not surprisingly, the family being the primary group, PCP work in family therapy shares many of the basic principles and aims described so far. Members learn to see things from each other's point of view, to clarify their views of themselves as distinct from those imposed on them by the family system. They may come to understand how their relationship with a parent or sibling has influenced other relationships and their dealings with situations outside the family have reflected situations which recur within it. Harry Procter (25) has worked and written extensively in this area. He has developed ideas of "family construct systems" and how they function and one of his aims in therapy is for members themselves to become aware of that system and perhaps challenge some of its workings.

PCP WITH GROUPS OUTSIDE THERAPY

Introducing his ideas for family therapy, Harry Procter sees them as just as applicable to other groups: "work and friendship groups, organisations and even transient acquaintanceships". If we substitute the terms "social construct" and "social construct system" for family construct and family construct system the relevance is clear. Groups of people working together in any setting will have constructs in common about what they are doing as well as highly individual notions of the tasks and purposes involved. The distinction between the two may not always be clear and misunderstandings arise when commonality is falsely assumed or individuality ignored. Unlike groups of therapy clients, awareness of such problems may be lacking.

Problem Solving in Business and Industry

In a book referred to earlier, edited by Fay Fransella and Laurie Thomas (32), we find examples of the use of PCP within business and industry. Joyce Watson describes a project in which a group of supervisors were involved with the aim of improving their standard of performance. They were seen individually as well as in a group. During the group sessions the members tested out the new ideas they had developed in individual sessions on one another. It allowed them "to experience a variety of ways of working that they might not have considered themselves, and to see the different interpretations of the new role" which they all felt they needed to adopt.

At the same PCP Congress on which this book was based Philip Boxer outlined his work with large organisations. His main theme was the conflicts which can exist when the organisation imposes certain "regnant" constructs on those who manage and work for it which the individual either misconstrues or finds confusing or antipathetic. Regnancy, which we described in Chapter 4, may be looked at in this context as the overriding ethos of a company, bringing with it an implicit set of "rules" and aims. Crisis can truly occur when some imminent change threatens to alter those regnant constructs and the employees from management downwards have to adjust to a new set of rules. He makes the interesting and crucial point that in organisations, as so often in life, you can't change things—you can only change your relationship to things. In his work with managers he helped them first to see what the organisational regnancy was, then to see where they stood in relationship to it and whether they were prepared to "shut up, put up" or would have to leave. Such decisions can of course be made through individual exploration but as with the project described by Joyce Watson, group sessions where individual findings can be tried out and exchanged have enormous potential.

Group Reconstruction in Education

With education going through a period of such upheaval at the present time, this kind of approach, where individual difficulties are exchanged compared and contrasted would seem potentially very helpful. A PCP orientation would provide the structure and process needed to resolve what must sometimes seem irresolvable confusion. Just as Tom Ravenette has shown that pupils and teachers can come to construe each others' constructions more effectively, so groups of teachers, school managers and staff, parents and teachers would benefit from sessions aimed at such mutual understanding. (Only a crazed optimist, perhaps, would envisage meetings between Government and Educationalists along these lines, but we all have the right to dream!)

After carrying out a research project for a large education authority on teachers' responses to a government scheme for encouraging self-development, the Centre for Personal Construct Psychology in London was asked by some of the teachers involved to run seminars and a workshop on PCP. It was clear that the experience of having their constructs about their work elicited and laddered had made them interested in this new way of looking at how they felt about things. Although not "group work" as such, these meetings involved not only learning about the approach but sharing their constructions particularly about education and the changes occurring in their field. This is not the first time that people involved in such projects have "asked for more" and found PCP to have wider meaning for them than their original encounter with it.

The Contribution of PCP to Groups So Far

Any group of people working together with the aim of changing things, whether it be themselves and their lifestyles, their work situation or the structure of an organisation, may go through some of the processes touched on, whether a PCP approach is used or not. In therapy groups of whatever kind, the therapist will need training and preparation and will come to the sessions with anticipations both of their role and of the other group members. Clients also will have expectations and purposes. So what especially has Kelly's psychology to offer to the group situation?

First, the therapists bring to their work a theory which is clear, strong and consistent in its formulation. Earlier chapters have spelt out the details, so there is no need for reiteration here. Like therapists from a number of other orientations, he or she will wish to understand how the members of the group experience things as closely as possible and to be aware of the changes occurring for the group as a whole as well as for individual members. The exploratory techniques can greatly facilitate this understanding and awareness of change. In groups where these procedures are carried out before the group sessions begin, clients too have a clear picture of where they stand, which must be of benefit to them. Changes can of course then be identified by the re-application of these procedures.

It has also often been pointed out that PCT allows for technical eclecticism in the conduct of therapeutic sessions and this has been shown to some extent in the groups we have described. Not only is the use of role play, with the Kellyan addition of role reversal, perhaps more effective with a group of people, but aspects of fixed role therapy at least may be planned by the group as a whole, several heads being better than two. With the group for people who stuttered we demonstrated the usefulness of the members eliciting and laddering each others' constructs in the interests of better understanding. The interpersonal transaction method is also something which belongs very much to the core of PCP group aims—the development of sociality. And all this by no means precludes the use of techniques from other approaches; the only guideline is that they should be chosen with a specific purpose in mind.

A further point might be added in relation to the effects of what goes on in the group on individual members. We and others have found that Kelly's way of looking at such emotions as threat, guilt and anxiety can make greater sense of seemingly negative reactions to challenge and change. Instead of seeing someone's refusal to cooperate simply in terms of bloody-minded "resistance", the therapist will look to what precious constructions of a particular member are being threatened, causing them, for the moment at least, to be hostile. If the important constructs are already known, then such threat may be anticipated and either prevented or, if it is considered more useful to be experienced, clarified and worked through when it occurs. If we consider anxiety as due to events being outside the range of convenience of a person's construing, then anxiety about what is going on in the group, which can be experienced by everyone concerned, including the therapist, will signify the need for clarification and modification of aims, perhaps before any progress can be made. Such anxiety may manifest itself in anger, obstruction, or someone's simply not coming back.

That no-one so far has found Kelly's "phases" of particular usefulness does not seem very important. The group processes described within those phases are phenomena to be encouraged, in whatever order they occur. One very striking thing in all this is the fertility of Kelly's ideas, which has led to many inventive procedures and methods developed since. While, as we have pointed out, some aspects of a PCP approach to working with groups can be found in other orientations, much of what we have discussed is unique and we believe makes a valuable contribution to group functioning. We have no doubt that developments in this area will continue and that the range of groups for whom it is found useful will widen still more.

12

WHERE DO WE GO FROM HERE?

If you have come thus far with us it is hoped that you will be interested in going on from here. But where do you *want* to go? Some of you may have been thinking of undertaking therapy but not know what to expect or hope for. Perhaps the approach outlined here appeals to you. If you are a therapist from some other background or trained to deal with specific disorders such as speech and language problems, or have a wider brief in the alleviation of distress as a social worker, perhaps, you may feel that PCP would enhance the work you do. We certainly hope that those of you involved in education or the care of children in some other form will have found the ideas relevant to the understanding of young people. And for those whose profession in business or industry is concerned with either the management of others or the processes of organisation, the aspects we have touched on here may make it seem worth your while to look more deeply into what PCP might have to offer you. Even if none of these descriptions apply to you, the ideas which follow may be of further interest.

Once again, we wish to stress that we do not intend to make any sharp distinction between "professionals" and "clients". Someone thinking of embarking on therapy at this time may well also be interested in the ideas professionally and any professional may at some point feel that they need help from another professional. It is also possible to see therapy as a learning process in itself. Some students at the Centre for Personal Construct Psychology have taken a Diploma course and been involved in PCP therapy at the same time. The headings below, therefore, may be seen as somewhat arbitrary.

TO PROSPECTIVE CLIENTS

Chapters 7, 8 and 9 should have given you a comprehensive idea about the approach to therapy and what your involvement might be if you decide to undertake it. If you have experimented with the suggestions given in Chapter 9 you will know whether or not it is enough to do it all by yourself. The disadvantages here were put forward and you may feel that you *do* need professional help. But perhaps you would like to read more about it too. The references at the end of this book are to all the work we have mentioned as we've gone along, but here we shall pick out just a few that we feel might be especially helpful to you.

Depression: the Way Out of Your Prison (Routledge, 1983). This is written by Dorothy Rowe, who until 1986 was District Psychologist in North Lincolnshire. She has done extensive clinical work with people who are depressed and although her ideas on depression and other topics have developed as a result of wide-ranging study and practice, the influence of Kelly's psychology has clearly been great. This is a very thought-provoking and readable book on the subject.

Personal Construct Theory and Mental Health (Croom Helm, 1985). Although written primarily for professionals, this book too, edited by Eric Button, some of whose work on eating disorders we have discussed, is also very readable. Particular chapters may appeal to people who feel they have a specific problem addressed in one of them. We have already referred to chapters on eating disorders, alcohol dependence, family therapy and mental handicap but there are also contributions on topics such as schizophrenia, neurotic disorders and drug dependence.

Finding a Therapist

This is not always easy and may depend on where you live. Although PCP is being chosen as an approach more and more, therapists are still thin on the ground in many areas. One useful source of information is the British Association for Counselling's *Counselling and Psychotherapy Resources Directory*. This can only be obtained by becoming a member of BAC, but if you contact any clinical psychology department in a hospital they should be willing to check through for you or may actually know of someone in the area who is working from a PCP perspective. Failing that, you could telephone BAC or write to them:

British Association of Counselling 37a Sheep Street Rugby Warwickshire CV21 3BX Telephone: 0788 78328

If there is no-one near you who works in this way, there is no harm in telling a therapist you meet and feel comfortable with of your interest. You may find it possible to use the suggestions given in Chapter 9 with his or her help. Or you could lend them this book! It would at least show how you feel you might best be able to make progress.

TO PROFESSIONALS

If you have not come across PCP before, you too may wish to read more. The books suggested for clients would be relevant for you and there are many more on the subject of therapy listed amongst the references. Again, though, we shall pinpoint one or two which we feel would be of particular interest to you.

Personal Construct Counseling and Psychotherapy (Wiley, 1984). Authored by Franz Epting, an American Professor of Counseling Psychology at the University of Florida. He studied with George Kelly while he was a graduate student at Ohio University and, among other things, has made developments in fixed role therapy.

Working with People (Routledge, 1988). This is edited by Gavin Dunnett and contains chapters by workers in a number of areas such as Social Work, Speech Therapy, Occupational Therapy, Clinical Psychology and Psychiatry. It may be useful for you at least to read what has been written about developments in your own field, but probably interesting, too, to see where PCP is going in other professions.

Personal Construct Psychology: Psychotherapy and Personality (Wiley, 1980). Jointly edited by Al Landfield, who also worked with Kelly, and by Larry Leitner, it contains chapters on the theory in relation to clinical work, on the processes of psychotherapy and on research.

Personal Construct Therapy Casebook (Springer, 1987). Edited by Robert and Greg Neimeyer, it has, besides an excellent overview of the theory and techniques, some detailed accounts of individual, marital, family and group therapy.

We hope, of course, that reading *this* book has given you some enthusiasm for the theory behind the practice and we recommend, above all, Kelly's own two volumes:

The Psychology of Personal Constructs (Vols. I & II, Norton, 1955). These would for the moment only be available from libraries as they are out of print. But they are soon to be reprinted by Routledge in conjunction with the Centre for Personal Construct Psychology in London.

Clinical Psychology and Personality (Krieger, 1969). This collection of Kelly's papers was edited by Brendan Maher and shows later developments of his ideas both in the theory and the processes of therapy.

Inquiring Man (3rd edition, Croom Helm, 1980). This is by Don Bannister and Fay Fransella, who have done more to bring PCT to the fore in Britain than anyone. In this book, which has been many people's introduction to Kelly, they discuss the theory and show what has taken place in clinical and other research.

Training for Professionals

Although we trust that reading this book will enable you to introduce new ways of approach into your work, if you really want to take on PCP as the major dimension of what you do, you will gain more from some kind of practical and theoretical training—certainly from working with others, rather than alone. We have spoken several times of the theory's essential reflexivity and we can all be reflexive on a desert island, of course. But that reflexivity is in itself encouraged when working with others. Understanding the theory is enhanced by discussion, and practical experience in using the exploratory techniques and methods for experimentation undoubtedly needs the presence of others. Although less available than training in some of the longer-established approaches, there are courses in PCP and, failing that, there are people who join together to pool their resources in more informal ways.

The Centre for Personal Construct Psychology

This Centre, founded by Fay Fransella, was set up almost a decade ago to train people in PCP, provide services to individual clients and groups and to do research. The Diploma in PCP (Therapy and Counselling) is a three-year part-time course involving group sessions for theoretical and practical study, supervision and a number of experiential workshops. Students must already have had basic training in one of the helping professions and some experience before they join the course. There are also modifications of the Diploma for those wishing to use the approach in Management, Education, Career Counselling, Research and other fields. Most of the courses and some of the workshops take place at the Centre, whose address is:

Centre for Personal Construct Psychology, 132 Warwick Way, London SW1V 4JD. Telephone: 071 834 8875.

Not everyone will be able to undertake this London-based training. And most of the people whose work we have referred to were using PCP before the Diploma was invented! So although, having been through it ourselves, we would highly recommend it, there are other ways of furthering your understanding and experience. Short introductory courses are held elsewhere and people do, as we have said, meet together in groups regularly or occasionally and have found these meetings helpful and encouraging as a resource for exchanging ideas and experimenting with them. Details of such activities can be found in *Constructs*, the Newsletter of the PCP Centre. Conferences and other gatherings with a PCP focus are to be found during the year, so it should be possible to make and maintain contact.

TO ALL PERSONAL SCIENTISTS

If you have skipped the first two sections because you don't see yourself either as a prospective client or a professional, may we suggest that you go back and read them after all? Some of the reading we have suggested is quite wide-ranging and may appeal to you. You may at some time want to point someone else in the direction of therapy or you could even become interested in taking a course in PCP without becoming involved in the work of the Diploma which we have outlined. A number of people go to the Centre on courses just because they want to know more about it all. Interest groups around the country are not necessarily restricted to those involved professionally.

So why do they come? Or why *are* people outside therapy and counselling so often struck by these ideas at all? What, for example, drew a historian, David Gillard (46) towards it and made him see the theory as a tool for his trade? He found that it not only helped him to understand some of the more controversial giants of the past but was a means through which to look at "political, social and economic changes" as a whole. Peter du Preez (47), whose interests are social and political, has looked at the apartheid situation in South Africa from a PCT point of view and found it enlightening. There have been a number of studies of religion using the theory. People whose passion is music or poetry have also found something here to throw light on these aspects of experience. There seems no end to the possible extension of these ideas.

But by far the most important application of the theory in our eyes is to that highly personal subject—ourselves. We have tried to share a little of how it has helped us (Chapter 6). Recently, more people have been willing to be *personal* about it in print, most notably, perhaps, Miller Mair (48) who writes of himself and his relationships with others and the events which have occurred for him in a way which is very unusual for its openness in the psychological literature. We have called this book *A Psychology for Living* and that, simply, is what we believe personal construct psychology to be. Not because it has some kind of magic power to make all well for us or some special laws for life which we feel we must follow. It has neither.

It is a way of looking at ourselves and the world around us which can help us to understand things better in our *own* ways, not anybody else's. Helping us, perhaps, to understand our own understanding, to make something new of what we are experiencing and something different of what we might become.

REFERENCES

References are presented in the order in which they appear in the text.

1. Kelly, G.A. (1955). *The Psychology of Personal Constructs*. Norton.
2. Kelly, G.A. (1979). *Clinical Psychology and Personality* (a collection of papers, ed. Maher). Krieger.
3. Neimeyer, R.A. (1985). *The Development of Personal Construct Psychology*. University of Nebraska Press.
4. Rowe, D. (1983). *Depression: The Way Out of Your Prison*. Routledge.
5. Hjelle, L.A. and Ziegler, D.J. (1981). *Personality Theories* (2nd edn). Magraw-Hill.
6. Rogers, C. (1951). *Client-Centred Therapy: Its Current Practice, Implications and Theory*. Houghton.
7. O'Reilly, J. (1977). The interplay between mothers and their children, in D. Bannister (Ed.), *New Perspectives in Personal Construct Theory*. Academic Press.
8. Bannister, D. and Fransella, F. (1986). *Inquiring Man* (3rd edn). Croom Helm.
9. Brierly, D.W. (1967). The use of personality constructs by children of three different ages. Unpublished doctoral dissertation. London University.
10. Salmon, P. (1970). A psychology of personal growth, in D. Bannister (Ed.), *Perspectives in Personal Construct Psychology*. Academic Press.
11. McCoy, M.M. (1977). A reconstruction of emotion, in D. Bannister (Ed.), *New Perspectives in Personal Construct Theory*, Academic Press.
12. Dunnett, G. (1985). Construing control in theory and

therapy, in D. Bannister (Ed.), *Issues and Approaches in Personal Construct Theory*. Academic Press.

13. Bowlby, J. (1980). *Loss, Sadness and Depression: Attachment and Loss*, Vol. 3. Penguin.

14. Viney, L. (1985). Physical illness: a guidebook for the kingdom of the sick, in E. Button (Ed.), *Personal Construct Theory and Mental Health*. Croom Helm.

15. Green, D. (1986). Impact on the Self. *Constructs* **4** No. 1.

16. Ravenette, A.T. (1987). Personal construct theory and practitioners who work with children. A PCP Centre Occasional Publication.

17. Powell, K. (1988). *Stress in Your Life*. Thorsons.

18. Dunnett, G. (1988). Enlarging horizons: personal construct psychology and psychiatry, in G. Dunnett (Ed.), *Working with People*. Routledge.

19. Dunnett, G. (1988) Phobias: a journey beyond neurosis, in Fay Fransella and Laurie Thomas (Eds), *Experimenting with Personal Construct Psychology*. Routledge & Kegan Paul.

20. Bannister, D. (1962). The nature and measurement of schizophrenic thought disorder. *Journal of Mental Science*, **11** No. 8, 825–842.

21. Button, E. (Ed.) (1985). *Personal Construct Theory and Mental Health*. Croom Helm.

22. Dalton, P. (1989). Working with mothers and their children: a personal construct approach. *Clinical Psychology Forum*, a BPS publication.

23. Dunnett, G. (Ed.) (1988). *Working with People*. Routledge.

24. Mancuso, J.C. and Handin, K.H. (1980). Training parents to construe the child's construing, in A.W. Landfield and L.M. Leitner (Eds), *Personal Construct Psychology: Psychotherapy and Personality*. Wiley.

25. Procter, H.G. (1987). Change in the family construct system: therapy of a mute and withdrawn schizophrenic patient, in R.A. Neimeyer and G.J. Neimeyer (Eds), *Personal Construct Therapy Casebook*. Springer.

26. Bannister, D. and Agnew, J. (1977). The child's construing of self, in A.W. Landfield (Ed.), Nebraska Symposium on Motivation 1976. University of Nebraska Press.

27. Jackson, S.R. and Bannister, D. (1985). Growing into Self, in

D. Bannister (Ed.), *Issues and Approaches in Personal Construct Theory*. Academic Press.

28. Maitland, P. (Ed.) (1988). *Personal Construct Theory, Deviancy and Social Work*. Published by Inner London Probation Service and PCP Centre.

29. Davis, H. and Cunningham, C. (1985). Mental handicap: people in context, in E. Button (Ed.), *Personal Construct Theory and Mental Health*. Croom Helm.

30. O'Connor, G. (1988) Counselling in industry. *Constructs*, **6** No. 2.

31. Porter, J. (1988) On the nature and management of stress. *Constructs*, **6** No. 3.

32. Fransella, F. and Thomas, L. (1988). *Experiments with Personal Construct Psychology*. Routledge.

33. Fransella, F. (1972). *Personal Change and Reconstruction*. Academic Press.

34. Mair, J.M.M. (1977). The community of self, in D. Bannister (Ed.), *New Perspectives in Personal Construct Theory*. Academic Press.

35. Slater, P. (Ed.) (1976). *The Measurement of Intrapersonal Space by Grid Technique*. Vols 1 & 2. Wiley.

36. Fransella, F. and Bannister, D. (1977). *A Manual for Repertory Grid Technique*. Academic Press.

37. Stewart, V. and Stewart, A. (1981). *Business Applications of Repertory Grid Technique*. Mcgraw-Hill.

38. Beail, N. (Ed.) (1985). *Repertory Grid Technique and Personal Constructs*. Croom Helm.

39. Tschudi, F. (1977). Loaded and honest questions, in D. Bannister (Ed.), *New Perspectives in Personal Construct Theory*. Academic Press.

40. Ravenette, A.T. (1977) Personal construct theory: an approach to the psychological investigation of children and young people, in D. Bannister (Ed.), *New Perspectives in Personal Construct Theory*. Academic Press.

41. Dunnett, G. and Llewelyn, S. (1988). Elaborating PCT in a group setting, in G. Dunnett (Ed.), *Working With People*. Routledge.

42. Dalton, P. (Ed.) (1983). *Approaches to the Treatment of Stuttering*. Croom Helm.

43. Hayhow, R. and Levy, C. (1989). *Working with Stuttering.* Winslow Press.

44. Landfield, A.W. and Rivers, P.C. (1975). An introduction to interpersonal transaction and rotating dyads, *Psychotherapy: Theory, Research and Practice*, **12**.

45. Alexander, P.C. and Follette, V.M. (1987). Personal constructs in the group treatment of incest, in R.A. Neimeyer and G.J. Neimeyer (Eds), *Personal Construct Therapy Casebook.* Springer.

46. Gillard, D. (1982). How to explain history. *Constructs*, **1** No. 2.

47. Du Preez, P. (1979). Politics and identity in South Africa, in P. Stringer and D. Bannister (Eds), *Constructs of Sociality and Individuality.* Academic Press.

48. Mair, M.M. (1989). *Between Psychology and Psychotherapy: a Poetics of Experience.* Routledge.

INDEX

Index compiled by A.C. Purton